Oxford Progressive English R
*General Editor: D.H. Hou*

Dragon Seed

10856

# MORETON HALL
## FICTION LIBRARY

The Oxford Progressive English Readers series provides a
wi.... ......... ...... ... English, including
cla.... the favourite stories of young readers, and also
m.... ....... The series has five grades: the *Introductory*
*Gr....* ... 1450 word level, *Grade 1* at a 2100 word level,
*Gr....* ... 2900 word level, *Grade 3* at a 3500 word level
and *Grade 4* which consists of abridged stories. Structural
as well as lexical controls are applied at each level.

Wherever possible the mood and style of the original
stories have been retained. Where this requires departure
from the grading scheme, glosses and notes are given.

All the books in the series are attractively illustrated.
Each book also has a short section containing questions and
suggested activites for stude...

# Dragon Seed
## Pearl S. Buck

Hong Kong
**OXFORD UNIVERSITY PRESS**
Kuala Lumpur Singapore Tokyo
1982

*Oxford University Press*

*Oxford London Glasgow*
*New York Toronto Melbourne Auckland*
*Kuala Lumpur Singapore Hong Kong Tokyo*
*Delhi Bombay Calcutta Madras Karachi*
*Nairobi Dar es Salaam Cape Town*
*and associates in*
*Beirut Berlin Ibadan Mexico City Nicosia*

*First published in Great Britain 1942 by Macmillan & Co Ltd*
*Second edition (Methuen & Co Ltd) 1949*
*Methuen Paperbacks edition first published 1976*
*This abridged and adapted edition first published 1982 by*
*Oxford University Press, © Oxford University Press 1982*
*OXFORD is a trademark of Oxford University Press*

*Abridged and adapted by Ellen O'Connor*
*Illustrated by Tomaz Mok*
*Simplified according to the language grading scheme*
*especially compiled by D.H. Howe*

*ISBN 0 19 581507 6*

*Printed by Astros Printing Ltd.,*
*8, A Kung Ngam Village Rd., Hong Kong*
*Published by Oxford University Press,*
*Warwick House, Quarry Bay, Hong Kong*

# Contents

Pearl S. Buck was born in 1892 in West Virginia, USA. She was brought up in China, where her parents were missionaries. After attending university in America she returned to China to be a missionary and teacher at Chinese universities. Of her many novels about China the best-known are *The Good Earth* (published in OPER Grade 3) and *Dragon Seed*. She died in 1973.

# *I*
## *Ling Tan and his Family*

Ling Tan stood in the water and looked out over the rice field. He heard the sound of his wife's loud voice. 'Why is she calling me in the middle of the afternoon, when it's neither time to eat nor sleep?' he wondered. He looked over to the farther corner of the field where his two sons were bending 5 over in the water, planting rice seedlings*.

'Is your mother calling me?' he asked.

'Yes, father,' answered the young men.

Ling Tan left the rice field and went in the direction of his wife's voice. 10

His two sons, Lao Ta and Lao Er, continued to work in the field. Both sons were already married, and the eldest, Lao Ta, had two sons of his own. Lao Er, the second son, had been married for four months and there was no sign of children. Ling Tan had a third son, Lao San, who was 15 almost sixteen years of age. There were also two daughters in his house, only one of whom was still to be married. He had given the elder daughter to a merchant's son in the city.

Lao Ta and Lao Er were good friends as well as brothers 20 and had always been so from the moment they could remember. There was less than a year between their births, and they always told each other everything. Today they talked about their wives.

'Jade and I have no children yet,' said Lao Er to his broth- 25 er. His voice was sad.

'In time brother,' laughed Lao Ta. 'Be gentle with the girl.'

Lao Er looked up at Lao Ta and laughed. 'Gentle? With Jade?' Lao Er said. 30

*seedlings, young plants grown from seed.

I

They laughed together, thinking about the young, quick-tempered girl who was Lao Er's wife. Lao Ta's wife, Orchid, was quiet and plump, and if she had a temper she kept it to herself. But Lao Er's wife was like a Western wind. Wher-
5 ever she was she stirred all around her. Lao Er loved her the moment he saw her.

Lao Er's wife was full of mischief. Lao Er never knew where she was until he had her safely beside him. Sometimes she disappeared for hours and when she returned she would
10 never tell him where she had been. Her name was Jade and Lao Er loved her with his entire soul.

As he worked in the field today, he thought of Jade's beauty and spirit and he loved her even more.

### The visitor

Ling Tan stood with his wife, Ling Sao, in their courtyard
15 listening to a stranger. He was a pedlar of Shantung silks and grass cloth and he had come down from the North to sell his goods to the farmers of the South.

Ling Sao turned the material over in her hands. 'Your price is too high, pedlar,' she said sternly.
20 'What? I have put the price at a gift because there is to be a war this summer in the North.'

Ling Sao dropped the cloth.

'What war?' she and Ling Tan asked.

'The war with the little dwarfs, from the East Ocean, who
25 always like to fight,' answered the pedlar.

'Will they come here?' she asked.

'Who knows?' he replied.

The pedlar went on to tell them what he knew of the war in the North.
30 'You say the East Ocean dwarfs have killed some of our people?' asked Ling Tan.

'In the North they have killed men, women and children,' he said. He drank the last of his tea. 'I must leave you now, as I have a long journey ahead. Thank you for the tea.'

He gathered his goods together and left Ling Tan and Ling Sao in the courtyard.

Ling Sao sat down to continue her sewing. Ling Tan stood and looked at his house. 'I am a lucky man,' he thought. 'I have my house of brick and tile where I was born. My  *5* ancestors were born in this same house, and here they died, as I will.' He smiled and thought, 'My land, my house and my family are my wealth.'

Ling Tan was neither rich nor poor. He, himself, had never been ill. At fifty-six his body was as slim and strong as it had  *10* been in his youth. He was lucky that his share of the land was near a great city, near the big river, in a valley set under hills, from which water ran down even in dry weather.

'I must go back to work,' he announced to Ling Sao.

## Back to the fields

In the field he was pleased to see how near his sons were  *15* to the end of the planting. Another good hour and by sunset the field would be done. This was the last field, and with it all his rice would be planted and his family fed for another year. He bent down beside Lao Er and began planting too.

Ling Tan could not read a word. He had never needed  *20* to read. He had not sent his sons to school either, and for this he was not sorry. He and his sons were farmers and they did not need to read to farm the land.

Ling Tan and his sons worked for the next hour. At last the final seedling was planted.  *25*

They stood straight and stretched their tired bodies.

'What did our mother want?' asked Lao Ta.

'There was a pedlar from the North and he brought news of a war,' answered Ling Tan. 'The North is far from here so there is no need for us to think of war.' And the three men  *30* turned and left the field for home.

Lao Er entered the house and went into the room which he shared with Jade. She was not there. He went to the kitchen and saw his mother feeding the fire.

3

'Mother, why do you feed the fire? My worthless wife ought to do it for you.'

'Worthless indeed,' said Ling Sao. 'I have not seen her since the sun was in the middle of the sky. These young
5 women! When I was a girl our feet were bound and we stayed at home. Now they run around like goats.'

'I will find her and bring her home and beat her,' said Lao Er.

'Good. Do it,' replied his mother. Lao Er left the kitchen
10 and Ling Sao continued to feed the fire. 'He will not beat her. What man would beat the beautiful Jade?' she sighed.

Ling Sao lifted the lid of the cauldron* and sniffed the rice. It was fragrant and nearly ready. She yawned and reach-ed for the rice-bowls which stood on a shelf on the earthen
15 chimney. Then she set the bowls on the table, put down the chopsticks and went into the room where she and her hus-band slept. He was there, washing himself with a bowl of cold water. She watched him wash, happy that she had a clean man.

20 Ling Tan saw her and said, 'Now I will have my supper.'

'Good,' she replied and she went to prepare the meal. She chopped the pork, rolled it into balls with garlic and salt and dropped the balls into boiling water. She looked at the rice again, and put the dried fish on the table. She
25 stood in the centre of the house and called, 'Your father is ready to eat.'

Lao Ta came and sat at the table with his youngest child in his arms. Ling Tan sat at the top of the table, smoking his pipe.

30 'Where is Lao Er?' asked Ling Tan.

'He is looking for his woman,' Ling Sao replied. Ling Tan and Lao Ta laughed because their wives never ran away.

Ling Sao and Lao Ta's wife, Orchid, waited on the men.

Soon the third son came quietly into the garden, leading
35 a water-buffalo by a rope through its nostrils. Lao San was

_____
*cauldron, large, deep pot with a lid used for boiling.

4

a tall, silent boy not yet sixteen years of age. He had a temper and some days he spoke to no one in his family. Ling Tan and Ling Sao let the boy do this because they loved him the best of all their children.

5 Lao San's face was beautiful. He was so beautiful that when he was born his parents were sure he would die. He had long eyes whose pupils were as black as onyx*. His face was square and his mouth was full. Because of his great beauty his parents forgave him everything. He washed his
10 hands and took his place at the table.

Ling Tan looked down the table at his sons. His heart was full as he thought of how very lucky he was in this life.

Ling Sao threw down an armful of straw for the buffalo
15 to eat. The yellow dog sat at Ling Tan's feet. Ling Tan bent down and gave him a handful of fish. Pansiao, the unmarried daughter, left her weaving loom and came to the table.

Ling Tan looked at his family again. 'I am a fortunate man,' he thought as he watched his family eat their meal.


### Lao Er and Jade

20 In the fields about the house, Lao Er was still searching for Jade. If she were there he would easily see her blue coat. The wheat was cut and the rice was still short so there was nothing to hide her. She was not there. 'Then she must be somewhere in the village,' he thought. He set off walking
25 towards the village, thinking of his marriage to Jade.

Lao Er had loved Jade the moment he saw her. But another man loved her and he too wanted Jade for his wife so her father put the whole choice upon which man's father gave the best price for Jade. The two young men begged their
30 fathers for money and threatened to kill themselves if they could not marry her. It was Ling Tan who had the answer to the problem.

*onyx, a kind of marble sometimes black in colour.

6

Ling Tan went to the other young man's father. He gave him thirty silver dollars to keep his son away from Jade. Then Ling Tan went to Jade's father and paid him as well. This was how Lao Er came to be married to the beautiful Jade. 5

Lao Er thought of all these things as he walked along the dusty road. And he thought of Jade's hair. Three weeks ago Jade cut off her shiny, waist-length hair. Lao Er had been so angry that he almost beat her.

'Why have you cut your hair?' he had screamed at her. 10

'Because I want to sell it to buy some earrings,' she had said with a laugh.

Because he loved her so much he had said, 'Jade, I will buy you some earrings.'

But Lao Er had not had the time to buy the earrings. 15 As he walked along this evening he thought that was why she had run away today.


### At the tea-house

He came to the village and looked in the shops as he walked down the main street. No Jade. He searched the crowd for her face and still there was no Jade. At last he 20 came to the village tea-house and here a crowd had gathered. A band of four or five young men and women were showing the crowd some magic pictures upon a sheet of white cloth they had hung between two bamboo poles.

Then the voice of the young man who had been speaking 25 came to Lao Er's ears.

'We must burn our houses and our fields. We must not leave so much as a mouthful for the enemy. There must be nothing for them here when they come. Are you able to do this?' he cried. 30

No one in the crowd spoke, they only stared at the picture on the white cloth. Now Lao Er looked at it too. The picture was of a city somewhere; of many houses and out of the houses came great flames and black smoke. Lao

7

Er watched as he saw one figure jump up. It was Jade.

'We are able. We can do it!' She cried in reply to the young man.

Lao Er was shocked. 'Jade,' he screamed, 'come home! I am hungry!'

She turned and saw her husband. She stood up, walked through the crowd and followed Lao Er.

When they were away from the crowd Lao Er said, 'Jade, why have you shamed me so in front of the village?'

Jade did not reply and she walked on behind him.

'How can I eat when you are not at the table?' he asked.

'If you are hungry you should eat,' she said.

'You know I cannot eat without my wife at the table,' he said, angrily.

They were away from the village now; on the way to the farm. Lao Er looked at her and saw that she was laughing.

'You treat me badly,' he said.

'You're a big turnip!' she said and laughed at him.

Lao Er turned and grabbed Jade into his arms. He pulled her close to him. 'I wish I was a man of learning,' he said in a soft voice.

'Why?' she asked.

'Because then I would have the words.'

'What words?'

'The words to tell you what I feel in me,' he said softly. Then he kissed her.

'I am not clever, either,' said Jade. 'You don't have to be clever to speak to me, Lao Er. You are always so silent. Two people must speak in order to understand each other.'

He held her close to him and thought about what she had said.

'Will you tell me everthing you are thinking if I tell you everything I am thinking?'

'Yes.'

'Then tonight we will speak together,' he said.

'Yes.'

*Back home*

They reached the farm and the family had almost finished their meal. Jade filled Lao Er's bowl and gave it to him before she took her place among the women.

Ling Sao spoke to Jade as she rose from the table. 'Since you did not cook the meal, you may clean up after it.'  5

'I will, my mother,' she said.

There was a little smile on Ling Sao's face. 'So my son must have beaten her after all,' she thought.

The meal was finished and Jade cleaned the kitchen. Lao Er waited for her to come to their room. At last they lay  10 beside each other in the darkness.

'Who will speak first, then?' he asked.

'You,' she said. 'Ask me what you will.'

'Did you really want me for a husband?'

'Is that what you wanted to know? Oh, Lao Er, the answer  15 is yes.'

'What do you think about all day?' Lao Er continued.

'I think of twenty things and thirty things at a time,' she said. 'My thoughts are like a chain and one leads quickly to others. I begin thinking about a bird and I wonder how it  20 flies and how it can lift itself above the earth and why I cannot. Then I think of the foreign flying ships and how they are made and why the foreigners know how to make them and we don't. And today I thought of what the young man speaking in the village said about the flying ships; how they  25 are crushing cities in the North.'

Lao Er interrupted her. 'Why did you go there today?'

'I wanted to hear what he had to say,' she answered.

'Sometimes I think you have a secret,' said Lao Er.

'Oh, Lao Er, I do. . . . Will you buy me a book? Instead  30 of the earrings, buy me a book. That is why I cut my hair off. I was going to buy a book but I was afraid to tell you so I lied and said I wanted some earrings.'

'A book! Why do you want a book? You cannot read.'

'Yes I can. I can read,' she said.  35

'You can read? Where did you learn?' asked Lao Er for

9

he was shocked to find that Jade could read. Farm girls were not educated and he knew she had not attended school.

'My father sent one of my brothers to school and from him I learned a little every day but I have no book of my own.'

'If this is what you want, I will give it to you, Jade,' he said.

And they continued to talk through most of the night, giving their thoughts to each other.

'We must sleep,' said Lao Er. 'Tomorrow I will go to the city and buy you a book.'

Jade smiled at Lao Er and held him in her arms. He loved her so much and now he knew she loved him. At last, his mind and heart were at peace.

## 2
# A Journey to the City

Now Lao Er often bought goods for his father, because of all three sons he was the one who was most at ease in the city. He was the son who did the city business, who took eggs to the corner shop at the Bridge of the South Gate, who weighed the pigs' meat when they were killed and who $5$ carried their surplus rice to the rice-shops after each harvest.

Today he walked into the city with his head up and his face clean. He was wearing a decent blue coat and trousers. He went to a certain street where booksellers had their wares set out on benches and he stared at them for a while. Some $10$ books were large and some small and to Lao Er they all looked the same.

The booksellers were small, old men who had once been scholars or teachers and who now sold books. They spoke to Lao Er as he passed by. $15$

'This is a good book, young man,' said one. 'I will give you a good price.'

Lao Er looked at the book. 'What is the title?' he asked.

'The title is what you see,' said the old man.

'The truth is I cannot read,' said Lao Er. $20$

'Why then do you buy a book?' asked the old man. 'Why don't you go and buy some sweets or a piece of cloth, you silly boy?' And he laughed at Lao Er.

### His brother-in-law's advice

Angrily, Lao Er turned away from the bookseller and walked on. 'I will go to my elder sister's house and if her $25$ husband is at home, I will ask his help on the book,' he thought. He knew his brother-in-law could read.

He walked down the crowded street and across three others and came to his brother-in-law's shop. It was a shop selling foreign stuff of all sorts; foreign flash-lights and rubber shoes and food in tin boxes and pens and pencils and pictures of white women with round, blue eyes. Today he went through the shop to the court behind, where his sister lived,

5 and found his brother-in-law.

Wu Lien was fat for his age because he drank and ate very well.

'Oh, my wife's brother,' cried Wu Lien. 'Come, sit down.'

Lao Er greeted his brother-in-law and sister. Then he told

10 them the news of the farm. Finally he said to Wu Lien, 'I wish to buy a book.'

Wu Lien had read many books because he was a city man and his father had sent him to school.

'Lao Er, first we must know why the book is wanted and

15 who is to read it.'

'The book is for my wife, Jade. She can read. She learned from her brother and now she wants a book of her own,' answered Lao Er.

'Which book does she want?' asked Wu Lien.

20 'I don't know,' said Lao Er. 'I thought all books were the same.'

'Oh, no. Each book tells a different story, Lao Er.'

Wu Lien thought about the situation for a moment then he turned to his wife. 'If you could read, what would you

25 like to read about?' he asked.

'Oh, I used to love listening to the stories of the robbers who lived by the lake.'

'Yes, I know what book those stories are from,' said Wu Lien. 'A very good choice, wife,' Then he turned to Lao Er.

30 'It has everything in it and all the women who deceive their husbands are punished and the righteous win. The name of the book is, "Shui Hu Chuan", and it is full of righteous robbers. That is the book to buy Jade.'

Lao Er repeated the name of the book, thanked Wu Lien

35 and his sister and left the store. Suddenly he heard the sounds of loud, angry voices in the street. He looked up and saw a band of young men a few shops away. They were

making their way towards Wu Lien's store.

In the front of the group was their leader, a tall young man who wore no hat and whose long hair fell over his eyes. He shouted at the shop assistant, in Wu Lien's store, to open the display case. When the assistant delayed, he took up a  5
rock in his hand and crashed it through the glass of the locked case.

'Enemy goods!' he cried in a high voice as he grabbed* watches and pens from the display case and threw them into the street. The moment he did this all the young men rushed  10
into the shop and began to break the cases and throw out the goods. They smashed them onto the ground, breaking them into small pieces.

Lao Er watched and his heart was sick at the waste of his brother-in-law's merchandise. He was half-way to the city  15
gate before he remembered that he had forgotten to buy his book. So he turned back to the street of booksellers and went to one table and asked for the book. The bookseller handed him an old, dirty book. 'A dirty book like this must be cheap,' said Lao Er, looking at the black, greasy spots on it.  20

'It might have been a few days ago,' the bookseller said, 'but in the past few days many students have come to buy this book. I don't know why.'

'What is the price?' asked Lao Er.

'Three small, silver pieces,' answered the bookseller.  25

'For a book?' said Lao Er, shocked at the expense.

'Why not for a book?' said the man. 'You spend as much on a piece of pig's meat and you eat it and it is gone. But a book you put into your mind and there it lies and you can read it over when you forget it and think about it again.'  30

So Lao Er reached into his pocket and gave the man the money for the book. He turned and walked down the street. He had not gone far when he thought he should go and see if his sister and brother-in-law were safe. He thought of the angry band of young men and he was worried.  35

*grabbed*, seized suddenly.

13

### The shop

When he reached their place the shop was boarded up and only a heap of ashes lay on the street. He stood there and asked himself if he should go inside and see if his sister was safe. But Lao Er knew his first duty was to his family and
5  that his father would be unhappy if his son was mixed up with this trouble.

The boards covering the shop had letters scrawled, in white chalk, all over them. He stared at the letters for a long time but nothing came to his mind. 'Now I wish I could
10  read,' he said to himself. An elderly, learned-looking man in a long, black robe passed Lao Er.

'Sir, will you tell me what these letters say?' he asked.

The man looked at the letters and was quiet for a moment. Then he turned to Lao Er and said, 'These letters say that
15  what has happened to this house shall happen to every house that sells enemy goods, and if this is not enough, life itself will be taken from those who sell or buy enemy goods.'

'Sir, thank you,' said Lao Er. The words frightened him and he knew that in duty to his parents he must leave this
20  spot and hasten to the safety of his own home.

With his book for Jade under his arm he left the city where such terrible things could happen.


### A book for Jade

When he arrived home he gave the book to Jade, but even the book was forgotten today because of what he had to tell
25  them. The whole family listened to his story of the band of young men and the writing on the boards of his sister's house.

When Lao Er had finished Ling Tan spoke. 'Did you ask what the name of this enemy was?'
30  'No father, I did not.'

But all that had happened in the city was very far from those who lived in this house. Night fell as it always did and they ate and made ready for bed as they did every night.

Ling Tan and Ling Sao talked together for a little while
before they slept.

'She is not of this house any more, and it is up to her
husband to protect her,' said Ling Sao of their daughter.
'If there is bad trouble she will get a message to us.' Then    5
she and Ling Tan fell asleep.

Lao Ta and Orchid talked of the evils of foreign learning.
'No child of ours will ever attend school!' said Lao Ta, and
then they slept.

Lao Er and Jade looked at the book. Jade opened it and    10
by the small light of the bean-oil lamp on the table she began
slowly to read aloud the characters. Lao Er watched her
pretty lips and listened to her lovely voice and he thought
it was magic.

'I love you, Jade,' he said, interrupting her reading.    15

She turned red and said, 'I love you too. And I am selfish
because I want you to learn to read and here I am reading
alone. Look at the characters with me.' And he did, then after
a while they fell asleep.

Of all the ones who lay in the house, only Lao San, the    20
third son, was thinking of what his brother had seen. 'Who
were the young men who destroyed his sister's shop? And
who was this enemy they spoke of?' he asked himself. He had
no answers and after many hours of tossing and turning he
finally fell into an uneasy sleep.    25

# 3
## The Land

as a man who lived his life both wide and deep,
thou.... seldom stepped off his own land. He did not
need to wander. He did not, as some do, own only the sur-
face of the earth. Ling Tan and his family owned the earth
5  under their land, and he used to think about this often.

He had once, in his youth, dug a well for his father and
for the first time he had seen what lay under the fields.
First there was the deep, thick crust of the earth and this
earth was so rich that anything planted in it sprung to life.
10 Under this earth was a hard, yellow bottom of clay, as tightly
packed as the bottom of a pan. And beneath that yellow
clay was a bed of rock, not solid, but splintered and split
into thin pieces, and between these was greyish sand.

Under this bed Ling Tan found pieces of tile and scraps
15 of blue pottery and an old silver coin. He had taken these
things to his father, and father and son had looked at them.

'These were used by our ancestors,' his father had said.
'Let us put them into the tombs with your grandparents.'

When they had done this, Ling Tan continued to dig and
20 soon water had sprung from the earth. 'But beneath this
water my land continues on,' he used to think.

It was a common saying in the village that if a man could
dig deeply enough in his own land he would find the roots
and ruins of what had once been great cities and palaces
25 and temples. Whether all this was true or not, Ling Tan did
not know. He did know that the land was his and all that
lay beneath it was his, and he was happy with these thoughts.

The whole earth, he had heard, was round. One day a
young man had come preaching in the village, telling of the
30 round earth. That the whole earth was round he found
hard to believe. What he could not comprehend was how, if
the earth were round, men on the bottom side would walk.

16

Ling Tan thought of these things as he tilled his earth, and it moved him to laughter to think that somewhere very far below the spot where he stood some foreigners stood, planting their seeds.

'I ought to ask them for my rent,' he would think and grin. One day Lao Ta and Lao Er asked him why he was grinning to himself.

'I have just thought that on the bottom of this land of mine, somewhere a foreigner reaps his grain without asking me, and that perhaps I should collect some rent from him.'

His sons laughed with him and soon the "foreigner" at the other end of their land became a family joke.

Sometimes Ling Tan thought about the future of his land. He thought of his three sons and their families and worried if the land could feed them all. He put the matter to his eldest son one day, not because he felt himself old and beyond work, but a man's years are lived when they are lived and there is a time for everything. Now was the time to plan and to think while his mind and body were still strong.

'Can this land feed three men and their wives and children after I am gone?' he asked Lao Ta.

'It can, for I will eat less meat if my brothers will and live in peace with them,' he answered.

Ling Tan was satisfied with the answer. He knew now he would leave the land to Lao Ta and that he would divide it equally among all, and this was fair.

Ling Tan and Ling Sao often talked about their children as they lay in their bed, late at night. Ling Sao was pleased that her two sons were married but she knew her sons loved her more than they would ever love their wives.

'That Orchid,' she grumbled one night in bed. 'She can do nothing but sit and look at her baby. Why, when I had a child it didn't stop me from working. Do you remember how I tended the fields and cut the wheat and harvested it *and* bore a second child?'

'There are not many women like you,' Ling Tan agreed, half asleep.

5

10

15

20

25

30

35

'And Jade,' Ling Sao sighed. 'What use is Jade to me? Her mind is on that book our second son bought her. Books! It was an evil day when a book came into this house, and there is nothing so bad for a woman as reading. I had rather
5 she took to opium.'

'No, not opium!' Ling Tan said, angrily.

'I didn't mean to say that, husband,' said Ling Sao. She knew how Ling Tan hated opium. At the age of forty-six his mother had begun to smoke opium to soften a pain in
10 her womb. Soon she cared nothing for food or clothing, but she had to have the opium. She lay with her eyes half shut night and day, dreaming and sleeping. This had gone on for seven years and more money had been wasted in the buying of opium than had been spent on food and
15 clothing. It had been a difficult time for all in Ling Tan's family and he hated the drug.

'And Pansiao, that little daughter of ours. What will we do about the weaving when Pansiao is married? Jade ought to learn the loom* in her place. I will tell her tomorrow.'
20 Ling Tan was fast asleep but Ling Sao continued to speak of her children. 'We must find a good, strong wife for Lao San. Although I said we need not worry about our eldest daughter, since she is no longer of this house, I *do* still worry.' Ling Sao was quiet for a moment. 'I know what I must do.
25 Tomorrow I will walk into the city and see her.' Ling Sao was now able to fall asleep.

## Ling Sao's journey to the city

The moment Ling Sao awoke she remembered what she had decided to do, and she rose long before any of the others awoke. She began to set the house ready for her
30 day's absence. By the time she was dressed and the house swept and the rice washed it was nearly dawn. It was still too early to light the fire, so Ling Sao went creeping into

*loom*, something used to weave thread into cloth.

18

the bedroom and brought out the little box where she kept her combs.

She started smoothing her hair which went into place on its own now so scarcely needed any oil; it lay so smooth by habit. She tied it with a strong, red cord, gathered it in a knot and twisted the knot over her long silver pin that had blue enamelled* ends.

When she had finished her hair and washed her face and rinsed her mouth it was time to cook the rice for the morning meal. Soon the others of the house awoke and came to the kitchen.

Ling Tan stared at his wife when he saw her.

'What is all this, mother of my sons?'

'I am going to see our eldest girl and find out how she and her family are,' Ling Sao said.

'How can you go to the city alone?' he asked.

Ling Sao tossed her head at this. 'Do I fear any man?'

She ate her food and called out to her daughter and sons' wives what they should do while she was gone. 'Orchid, tie your son to your back and prepare the food for this house. Jade, you shall keep the fire going for her. And Pansiao, you weave as you always do, but if your father wants anything you are to fetch it for him. Do not prepare any food for me, for I shall eat well at our daughter's house.'

Ling Tan went to their room and brought out some money for her to spend.

'Oh, no, why should I waste our good silver? I don't need it.'

But Ling Tan pushed it towards her, laughing, and in the end she took it, as he knew she would.

At last she was ready to go. She tied six hens' eggs and a few ripe peaches into a white handkerchief for her daughter.

The sun was well up over the mountain when she set out. She was looking forward to visiting her daughter.

---

*enamelled, covered with a smooth hard coat of glass.

*The city*

It was still so early that every now and then she passed a neighbour carrying his vegetables or straw to the city markets. And every now and then one shouted to her to ask how she was and how her husband was and where she was going.
5 To everyone she answered cheerfully and asked about them too.

She came to the city and made her way through the streets to her daughter's house.

The shop was open and the two assistants were there,
10 but not all the cases were full nor was all the glass mended. She went about looking for what used to be there and she saw that much of it was gone. What was left was cloth and small goods which could be bought in any little village shop. All the brightly-coloured, foreign things were gone.

15 She went to the back of the shop and found worse than she had feared. Her daughter's husband was sitting back in his chair, his fat was gone and he looked as though his skin were a garment too big for him.

'Oh, mother,' cried the daughter when she saw Ling Sao.
20 'Look at my husband. He cannot eat!'

Now Ling Sao knew very well that when a creature cannot eat his food he is on his way to the grave, and she was frightened at the thought of her daughter as a widow. She rolled up her sleeves and went to the kitchen.

25 Out of the eggs she had brought and some pieces of meat and onion she found in the kitchen, she made a dish so fragrant with goodness that Wu Lien smelled it, and opened his eyes.

Ling Sao took the dish to Wu Lien and said, 'Eat, now.'
30 He gripped the bowl in his hands and a few moments later brought the bowl down from his mouth, empty. Ling Sao and her daughter laughed. 'Now you are well,' she said to Wu Lien. 'Tell me of this trouble.'

'The nation will fall,' said Wu Lien, weakly.
35 'What do you mean? The nation is nothing but people and we are the people. You had one day of bad luck, and you

say that the nation will fall? Wu Lien, you go and buy more goods for this store.' Ling Sao stared at Wu Lien.

'I have bad news for you all,' announced Wu Lien, even though he knew that his wife and her mother would not understand what he was about to say. 'This is bad news for the nation. The East Ocean enemies have sent their ships to the coast nearest us. Their soldiers have stepped upon our land and our soldiers have met them but we are not strong enough for them.'

'Oh, Wu Lien, comfort yourself,' Ling Sao said. 'The sea is very far away and even the river is far enough. What can they do to us?'

'They have flying ships that can come up from the sea in two hours and lay their eggs down on us and burst our houses apart,' he cried.

Ling Sao looked at Wu Lien and thought his head might be a little soft for lack of food. 'The sea is far away,' she thought, 'and he is talking nonsense.'

Wu Lien knew the truth. He had read the newspapers from the coast and they had told of death and destruction. He also knew that his wife and Ling Sao had lived their whole lives in this area and that they did not read one word. 'How can they understand what is coming?' he asked himself as he watched them play with the children. 'They will understand soon enough!' His eyes filled with tears. 'And I am considered a traitor because I sold foreign goods. I am ruined for life.'

Ling Sao and her daughter played with the children during the afternoon. At last the end came to a very pleasant day for Ling Sao and she made ready for her walk home again. She thanked Wu Lien for his hospitality and bade her daughter farewell.

It seemed to her that the city had never looked so prosperous as it did this evening. The shops were full and busy. The streets were noisy with vendors and the people came and went laughing and talking. 'All is well in our country,' she said. 'Wu Lien talks of foolish and silly things.'

She went on home and at home she found them waiting for her, and each one had done as she had told them. The family sat together and talked and they listened to her stories of the grandchildren. In all her talking of the children she forgot to tell them what Wu Lien had said.

She was tired and she and Ling Tan settled in their bed. And so even to him she forgot to speak of war.

# 4
## The Flying Ships

How then could Ling Tan be prepared for the next day?

It was a day like any other it seemed, and so the family sat down to their morning food, and he directed each of his sons to his task for the day.

There was no other difference. The day was clear and the sky cloudless. He would plough today and plant tomorrow, and the next day there might be rain. 5

So he went out to his work and his sons went with him and in the house the women set themselves to their tasks. As he pushed the plough his eyes wandered up and down the valley and he saw in every field men like himself and his sons. They were his neighbours and his friends at work. 10

Then how could he be prepared for what he saw? It was mid-morning that he heard the noise of flying ships. He knew the noise for now and again he had heard it. Never had it been so loud as this. He looked up and he saw the sun shining upon the silver creatures in the sky. There were many of them and they moved with such grace as he had only seen before in wild geese, flying across the autumn sky. 15

In a moment they were all but over his head. He had stopped as soon as he saw them and so had every other man working on his land. They stood, their faces turned upwards, not in fear but only in wonder at such speed and such beauty. They all knew that these were foreign things, for none but foreigners could make machines like them. 25

Then they saw a silver fragment come out of one and drift down while the ships went on. The silver fragment dropped, slanting a little towards the East, and it fell into a field of rice. A fountain of dark earth flew up and this they all saw, still without any fear or knowledge. They ran towards the field, Ling Tan and his sons among the rest, to look for the 30

23

thing that had fallen. They could not find it. They did find
one or two bits of metal and a very large hole. The man who
owned the field laughed as he stared down at the hole.

'I have wanted a pond on my land for ten years and never
5   had time to dig one. Now here it is,' he said, laughing.

So busy were they that it was not until their first wonder
was over that they thought to hear and to see what was
going on now. One man did hear the same sounds over the
city, and he looked up and saw the city wall, a good three

miles away. Rolling smoke rose above the wall and curled upwards like black thunder-clouds.

'Now what?' said Ling Tan, but no one answered, for none knew. They all stood together and watched. They counted eight explosions inside the city wall and as for the flying ships, they thought them lost in the flames. They waited for a long while and when nothing else happened, they turned and went back to work.

No one took the time to go to the city that day and see

what the smoke was. By sunset the smoke was pale and all but gone. They went home to eat and to rest before the next day's work.

Ling Tan and his sons went home. At the supper table they laughed together about the man who had a pond dug easily on his land.

Late that night Ling Tan heard the yellow dog growl. He heard the noise at the gate grow louder, and by this time the whole house was awake and they all went to the gate together.

They heard a voice speaking and to their surprise it was the sound of a woman's voice.

'Are my father and mother dead, too, that they hear nothing?' These were the words that came loud and clear in the darkness of the night. As soon as they heard what was spoken they knew whose voice it was and Ling Sao ran forward.

'It is our eldest daughter!' cried Ling Sao. She threw open the gate and what she saw made her cry out.

There stood the eldest daughter and Wu Lien, each with a child, and there was old Wu Sao, Wu Lien's mother. They carried a few bundles of clothing, a teapot, some bedding, a basket of dishes and their kitchen god.

'We are all but dead,' the eldest daughter cried. 'The two servants and our two clerks lie buried in the ruins. The shop is half gone. We have nothing but our lives.'

Ling Tan could not understand what had happened. 'Why were the city gates not locked, to keep out those who did this?'

'How can the city gates be locked against the sky?' Wu Lien asked.

'What do you mean?' Ling Tan asked him.

'The city was bombed — have you heard nothing?'

'Bombed?' Ling Tan repeated. The word was one he had never heard.

His daughter went on. 'The flying ships came over the city this morning. I was feeding the baby and I heard the noise.

I jumped to my feet and I heard screaming everywhere. The shop, father and mother, the shop trembled and the north wall fell into a heap. Half our goods and the two shop assistants are buired there.' She stopped the story as her crying prevented her from finishing.                                    5

Ling Sao did not fully understand what her daughter was speaking of, so she cried out, 'We shall find beds for you. And Jade, you must light the fire for tea. In the morning we can set ourselves to understanding what is wrong.'

But Jade knew better and she said not a word but went   10
into the kitchen and Lao Er followed her.

'Is it not they?' she asked him quietly.

'Who else?' he said.

'It means our land is lost and our cities taken,' she said.

'It means that we may all die,' said Lao Er. He couldn't   15
bear to think of Jade's body dead and he put his arms around her.

'Why is it that we have not what all others in the world have?' Jade cried. 'Why have we not got guns and flying ships?'                                                             20

'They are of no worth to people like us who love only to live,' Lao Er answered.

They lay awake long into the night, thinking of what was to happen to their land and their bodies and their family.

*A new day*

In the light of morning the family sat around the table   25
speaking of what had happened yesterday.

Finally, Ling Sao understood what the bombs were and what they did to houses. 'And what about the people?' she asked.

'Into pieces,' Wu Lien replied, 'as though they, too, were   30
made of clay. Here an arm, there a head, there a piece of foot, a heart, and bits of bones, everywhere.'

Then there was silence.

'But why?' Jade asked.

'Who knows?' Wu Lien said.

In silence each family member rose and went at last to his task; the women to preparing the food and Ling Tan and his sons to the field, as they did each day of their lives.

5 That day passed and there were no flying ships. Nor the next day, nor the next. In their ignorance, Ling Tan and his family believed that the ships were finished with them, and that they would come no more. Three days later Ling Tan and Lao San, his youngest son, walked to the city to see the
10 destruction for themselves.

### The bombing

Ling Tan and Lao San set forth and soon they approached and entered the South gate of the city. At first they saw nothing to tell them what had happened except the grave* looks of the people who passed them by.

15 This city was a place famous for the gaiety* of its people. It was an old city, a place where for centuries rulers had lived and enjoyed fine food and beautiful women.

So Ling Tan and his son went to the first tea-shop and asked the waiter, 'Where is the ruin?'

20 The waiter cried out loudly, 'I had a little house of earth and straw and it is gone and all those in it but me. I had two fine sons and they are dead.'

Ling Tan comforted the man as he thought of what he had just told him. Then he and Lao San went to see for
25 themselves. They reached a street that was full of bricks and mortar and beams and dust. Upon these heaps some people dug with their hands and hoes. One woman found a foot and pulled it from the ruin, crying, 'It is my husband's foot, oh.'

30 Ling Tan turned and saw his son, vomiting.

'Yes, son, vomit for it is too much to bear,' he said sadly.

One young man climbed to the top of the heap of ruins.

*grave, serious. *gaiety, cheerfulness.

'You who love our country,' he said, 'listen to me. Yesterday the enemy flew over our city and dropped the bombs which destroyed houses and shops and killed men, women and children. The war has begun. We must fight the enemy. We must resist until we are dead, then our sons will resist. They    5
have taken the first hundred miles of our land, but we must not let them take the second hundred miles. Fight! Fight!'

The crowd shouted, 'Good!'. Ling Tan and Lao San joined in the cry.

As they shouted there came from the East the sound that   10
these people knew well, the sound of the flying ships. 'Hide yourselves,' shouted the young man.

Ling Tan and Lao San ran back to the tea-shop, and there they crouched* under a table. Now Ling Tan knew what was happening. He understood. The sound roared and their ear-   15
drums swelled and they could not breathe. They heard screams in the streets and the pain and fear seemed to last forever.

Suddenly it was over as quickly as it had begun and Ling Tan and Lao San were still alive.                                 20

Ling Tan and Lao San left the tea-shop and their eyes were filled with horror at the scenes in the city streets. Flames danced everywhere. People wailed and screamed. Houses were ruined. He took his son by the arm and they fled the city, leaving by the south gate.                           25

*Home*

They felt better as they saw the fields of green and brown before them. They spoke not a word but walked quickly, reaching the farm and the safety of their loved ones. But Ling Tan knew that no one was safe.

He gathered the family around the table.                      30

'I cannot save you,' he said aloud. 'Today we saw with our own eyes what Wu Lien told us about before. We have

*crouched*, stood with legs bent close to the body, hiding from something.

nothing but our bare flesh to fight against this enemy.'
He told them of the death and destruction they had seen.
'We can only bear what is to come and live on if we can,
and die if we must.'

5     Then Lao Ta said, 'There are only two things which can
be done when fire comes down from heaven. One is to escape
it by running away and the other is to let it come down and
bear it. I am staying here.'

'But I,' said Lao Er, 'will escape it.'

10     'If I were a man with no land, I would do the same,' said
Ling Tan. 'I only ask that you return to us when the war is
over.'

'I promise that,' said Lao Er.

The family spoke of what might come of them. As for
15 Lao San, no one asked what he thought and he said nothing.
He thought of what he had seen in the city and plotted*
how to seek revenge on this enemy.

The next day the flying ships came back again and the day
after that, and again on the next day. Every day they came
20 back. The city was scourged* by death and fire.

Ling Tan did not go there again. The family stayed where
it was and they tended their crops and put their food by for
the winter as they did every year.

Now, when the ships came over their heads they left the
25 field and hid themselves in the bamboo. For one day a flying ship had dipped low like a swallow over a pool, and cut
the head clean from a farmer who stood staring at it. Then
it had gone on again as though what it had done was play.

---

*plotted*, planned secretly.   *scourged*, beaten down by something.

30

# 5
## *The Beginning*

When all could see that death was to come every day, those
who lived inside the city walls did two things. They filled
the temples and prayed to the gods for rain as the flying
ships could not come in the rain. And they went out of the
city to find rooms in small country inns or a corner in a      5
farmer's house or they slept somewhere under a tree.
Never had Ling Tan seen such sad sights as he now saw.
Women and children and old people carrying all they could
tied up in bundles. Most of them travelled on foot, for
only a few of the rich could ride these days.                  10
These people were now the rich and poor together and
they did not know if ever they could go back. Sometimes
Ling Tan felt more sorry for the rich than the poor because
the rich were so helpless and delicate and knew little of
where to find food. The poor did better than the rich as they  15
were used to too little always.
The people poured into the countryside like a flooding
river. They were joined by the stream of people from the
East. As, foot by foot, the enemy took the land, the people
flowed inland.                                                 20
At first Ling Tan let his house be open to these people.
There were the wounded and the little children who could
not go on any further, and many died. None of these people
stayed long at Ling Tan's house because none of them
thought the house was far enough from the enemy. The         25
people wanted to go beyond the river and the lake and
mountain where the enemy dared not go yet.
Lao Er had decided that he and Jade would go, and so day
after day they waited until there came by those with whom
they wished to travel. They waited until one day a party of   30
forty young men and women came by. Jade liked them as
soon as she saw them. Their hair was cut very short, like

hers, and they all had books in their bundles.

'We are students of a certain school,' they told her, 'and our eyes are on the mountains a thousand miles from here where our teachers have already gone.'

5 Not one of these young men and women talked about wasting themselves in war, and this pleased Ling Tan very much. 'Those who have no learning have only their bodies and they are the ones who ought to fight if there must be fighting. But you who have wisdom stored in your skulls, you
10 have a treasure which ought not to be spilled like blood,' he said to them. Then he asked them many questions and for the first time he found out what had happened on the coast.

Lao Er came to him in the middle of the afternoon and told him that he and Jade wanted to go with this group. Ling
15 Tan understood and went to speak to Ling Sao.

She had never liked the idea of her second son and Jade wanting to leave their house. 'I do not see why Jade should go off like this,' she said angrily. 'She is expecting a child as you know, and that child should be born in this house.'

20 Ling Tan answered her with grave words. 'It may be better that we have very few young women in our house. The fewer the better. Jade is too beautiful for what may lie ahead of us.' For he was troubled by what one young man had told him in private about what had happened to some women at
25 the hands of the enemy.

'I don't want her to go,' said Ling Sao.

'I don't either, but a woman should be with her man and Lao Er wants to go,' Ling Tan answered.

### Lao Er and Jade leave

Ling Tan went into his house and told his son quietly that
30 he had better go and take Jade with him. He knew from what the young men had told him that the second hundred miles of land had been lost to the enemy and their house stood within the third hundred miles.

'But Lao Er, send me word somehow when the child is

32

born. If it is a boy send me a red cord in the envelope and if it is a girl let it be a blue one,' said Ling Tan.

'I will do better than that,' Lao Er replied proudly. 'Jade can write enough to tell you.'

'Can she?' said a shocked Ling Tan. 'Good, I will wait to *5* hear.'

Lao Er went to their room and there stood Jade, already prepared for the journey. She had tied a pair of straw sandals over her cloth shoes and she had put on her strongest, plainest, blue garments, such as country women wear; a *10* jacket and trousers.

'I am ready,' she said. 'Let us go.'

They went out and bowed to Lao Er's father and to his elder brother and they said farewell to all the others. But they could not find their mother anywhere, and since the young *15* men and women were anxious to be gone they had to leave without seeing her.

'Tell my mother we searched everywhere for her,' Lao Er said.

'I will,' said Ling Tan. He did not tell his son the thoughts *20* in his soul, when and if they ever meet again. He simply followed his son and Jade out of the gate and stood to see them go, and with him were all his household except his son's mother.

He spoke to Jade. 'Do your duty, child,' he said. 'Remem- *25* ber he is my son and his child is my grandchild and that all rests on you. When the woman is faithful no evil can happen. The woman is the root and the man the tree. The tree grows only as high as the root is strong.'

And so he let them go, and he stood looking after them *30* for a long time; as long as he could see them. Until their two figures were lost among the crowd.


*Ling Tan prepares for war*

When Ling Tan came into the house he saw smoke rising out of the kitchen and he went and looked behind the stove and there sat his wife, feeding grass into the fire.

'Where were you?' he cried. 'We looked for you every-where.'

'I couldn't come and watch them go,' she said.

5 'You have been weeping,' he said, staring at her. Her eyes were red and the tears had left silvery streaks down her brown cheeks.

'I have not,' she said. 'The smoke makes my eyes red.'

He let her say this, seeing the tears build up in her eyes
10 again, as he stood there helpless to ease* her sadness.

It seemed strange that two people could be so missed as Ling Tan and his wife now missed their second son and Jade. There were all the others left but it seemed some sort of strength had left the house with their going.

15 One evening soon after they had left the house, Ling Sao spoke of Jade. 'I never thought I would say I miss that girl, but I do. Of course, I long for my son much more. I do grow weary of Orchid. She does nothing if I do not tell her.'

20 'Ah, dear wife, so you *do* care for Jade.' said Ling Tan, smiling.

'Not much!' said Ling Sao.

'Do you know why you do not like Jade?' he asked to tease her.

25 'I know all I care to know,' she said.

'You do not know this, wife,' he said. 'You and Jade are alike!'

'What? That Jade!' she cried, trying to be angry. But secretly in her heart she was pleased, for Jade was beautiful
30 and she knew against her wish that the girl was an extra-ordinary one.

'Both of you are stubborn, wilful women and it is the only sort I like,' he said. 'Ought we not to understand our son and Jade? They are like us.'

35 'Yes, you are right,' she said, smiling at the truth of it all.

*to ease*, to make less painful.

34

As day followed day, they grew used to the two gone, and work went on. Ling Tan took the youngest son, Lao San, to the field with him to take Lao Er's place. Orchid was happy that Jade was gone for she had no use for the beautiful girl. Pansiao was sorry Jade was gone, for in the last few weeks Jade had taken a while in the evening to teach her to read a few characters. And the silent, little Pansiao loved learning them.

Now that was over, and Jade was gone, and Pansiao could only go over and over the characters she knew. One day, in her hunger to know what others said, she drew near to some of the women students who passed by the farm and asked them to teach her some characters. And by this means she learned to read a little. Then one day a kind student gave her a book from the few she carried. Pansiao thanked her and took the book, and she went through it with a piece of charcoal and marked every character she knew. But she did not know enough to understand the story of the book, and she made it her goal to read that entire book some day.

Day after day the flying ships came over, and the family grew used to them. Half of the city went away and then another third of those left, until only those stayed who had nowhere to go, or those who said it made no difference to them who ruled the city as long as there was peace. And mile by mile the enemy armies drew closer and city after city fell into their hands.

There was no news from those cities and no one knew whether the enemy was cruel or good, and all waited.

Ling Tan waited, too, but while he waited the work had to be done. He could not always be running into the bamboos because there were flying ships above his head. Yet, he did not want to risk his life and stay alone in the fields and tempt the enemy above to kill him. So he and his neighbours tied branches on their hats and looking down from above, a man in a flying ship would only see green, for their straw hats were large and the branches covered their blue trousers.

Ling Tan knew that the enemy was coming nearer because

35

he asked those people who fled and stopped at his farm for a rest. Day by day these people came from places nearer and nearer to him, and at last people came from the cities that he knew. This told him that the armies of the enemy were
5   winning.

'Do our armies fight these invaders?' he always asked, and the answer was always the same.

'Our men retreat to save themselves for a greater battle somewhere,' the people said, but no one knew where.

10   Ling Tan began to make himself and his house ready for the time when the enemy would rule over them all and under this rule they must somehow live.

Was the enemy good or evil? He could not find the answer as often as he asked those who came by. He thought of this
15   every day as he worked under the green branches tied to his hat and as the flying ships came and went over his head.

*Autumn*

'I will do my own work as I always have,' he thought. So the summer passed into autumn, and the harvests that year were all they had promised to be. The rice was heavier
20   than Ling Tan had seen in ten years, and the harvest so great that everywhere in this rich valley the people could barely* collect it all. The men of the valley put all their thoughts on the harvest and when soldiers came to them and asked them for help in digging trenches about the city, they sent
25   them away.

Ling Tan, like all others in his valley, despised* all who took part in war. He had no respect for these men who wanted to kill and fight with others.

Now while the grain was to be cut and threshed* Ling
30   Tan pressed everyone in his house into the work except Wu Lien, who could not learn how to hold a scythe. But

---

*barely*, hardly.   *despised*, felt someone to be without value.   *threshed*, separated the grain from the corn plant.

36

his wife remembered, as she had grown up on this farm and she went to the fields instead of Wu Lien, and worked as hard as any man. Wu Lien was ashamed of this.

'Wife,' he said angrily one day, 'am I just a sitter for the children?' 5

And his wife laughed at him which made him very angry and he hit her across the mouth until it bled.

'Who feeds you if it is not my father, and why shouldn't I harvest a little food to help him?' she screamed and went at him with her ten finger nails. 10

Ling Sao heard the yelling and went into their room. When she saw what was happening, she pulled her daughter away from Wu Lien and cried out, 'You shame me, daughter!' Then she turned to the scratched Wu Lien and said, 'I apologize for my daughter. Please forgive her.' And she took him 15 to the kitchen and made him a pot of tea.

She returned to the bedroom and her daughter told her what had happened. They laughed together and Ling Sao said, 'I take your side but you must remember that he is very ashamed of having lost his business and of being in this 20 house. Be patient with him.'

Her daughter knew her mother was right and she went to the kitchen and apologized to Wu Lien and all was well.

That night Ling Sao told Ling Tan the whole story and they laughed together. But Ling Tan knew that nothing must 25 come between a man and his wife, so he forbade his elder daughter to come into the fields any more. Thus, Wu Lien was a happier man.

The rice was harvested and a farmer with as much land as Ling Tan could store all his grain for the winter and still 30 have much left. It had to be sold and the people left in the city needed food too. Against his will Ling Tan had to go to the city to sell some of his harvest, and now he missed his second son, for he could send no one else and he had to go himself. 35

He waited until there was a rainy day when he knew the flying ships would not come and he walked through the mud

37

to the city. It was a sad day. Since he had seen it last the ruins in the city had grown much worse and all those left in the city had the look of tragedy on their faces.

5 He went to the rice-markets and sold his extra rice at a great profit. Yet any news he heard was not good, and the worst of all was that at last even the white foreigners were leaving the city too. When he heard this news he knew the worst was near.

10 'The foreigners always know what is going to happen before we do,' Wu Lien had told the family last night.

'How is that?' asked Ling Tan.

'They catch the news from the air and they run words along wires,' Wu Lien had replied.

'Magic,' Ling Tan said when he heard of this.

15 So today when he heard they were leaving, he knew the worst was coming. When he returned home he told the family the latest news. On every rainy day in the next few weeks he carried his extra rice to the city and sold it. And each time he visited the city the news was worse.

20 One day he began to look at the strength of his gate, and the fastening of its hinges*. He mended old holes in his walls, and he closed the small window in the kitchen. He made up his mind that if the enemy came, he would put all his family inside and he would be the only one to show

25 himself. He was frightened and he counted every hour as a man who knew he was going to die would count.

He bought beautiful gifts for each one in his family, for their faces were more dear to him now than ever before. Who knew if he would ever have the chance to buy them gifts of

30 love, again?

---

*hinges*, moving parts which let a gate or door open.

38

# 6
## *Waiting for the Enemy*

Early in the eleventh month the enemy was near the city. If Ling Tan lifted his head as he worked in a field he could hear the sound of battle. One day someone coming back from the city said that the terrible noise they heard was the huge foreign guns of the enemy.                                        5

The stream of those who fled had stopped. All who could go were gone, and only those that had to, stayed. Ling Tan made himself busy all day with the winter's work, and at night he sat and made straw sandals from the strong rice straw.                                                                        10

On the seventh day of that month the last of the rulers had left the city. There was an army left in the city to fight the enemy when it came, but what army would be brave when its rulers were gone? For twenty miles all around the city the villagers armed themselves with knives and ancient   15 swords, their pitchforks and old guns. They were ready to defend themselves against their own retreating armies, for they all knew what defeated soldiers did to everyone no matter what flag they were attached to.

Ling Tan armed himself with an old broadsword* which     20 had belonged to his grandfather. He and Ling Sao polished it as they listened to the roars of the great guns which were so close now that sometimes the dishes on the table would jump.

In the last few days, the worst news Ling Tan had heard came from the villagers nearest the city. For Ling Tan and his  25 kin* were lucky in that their village was a little more than three miles from the city. Within two and three miles the defending soldiers had burned the villages to prevent the enemy from plundering* them. Now the farmers came by the

---

*broadsword, a sword with a wide blade. *kin, family; relatives. *plundering, robbing by force in time of war especially.

Ling village and Ling Tan asked them why they were leaving their land.

'Our houses and our harvest are burned. Our land is now only scorched* earth. Why should we stay?' they said, and they hurried away.

Ling Tan went out and looked at his own land. 'If I could roll up the land and take it with me, then I would go. But my land goes deep under the skin of the earth and I cannot burn it or give it away. I will stay,' he said to Ling Sao.

'I will stay with you,' she answered.

Days passed and the noise of battle increased by the hour. On the tenth day of that month it was known that the enemy would come in three days.

Ling Tan locked his gate for now robbers and bandits* roamed the Ling village in search of women and food. They beat on his gate but Ling Tan had made it strong enough that they would beat for a while then run off to another house.

'I know they will rule over us when they come, but are they a kind ruler? Do they want law and order? If so, we can live under them,' Ling Tan said to himself over and over as he waited to see this enemy.

The ninety-year old elder of the village said from his long wisdom, 'What ways do we know but our own? Let us do as we should for any new people coming to our village.'

All listened to him and they agreed that what he said was right.

They decided that when the enemy came they would go out to greet them and that tea should be prepared and small cakes and fruits made ready for them.

In those next days while they waited there were those who went to the city and bought small enemy flags of paper for the people to hold in their hands when they went out to welcome the enemy. In hope and fear all waited.

---

*scorched*, burnt brown. *bandits*, people who rob and murder.

*The messenger*

Then came the thirteenth day of the eleventh month. That morning when Ling Tan rose he knew what day it was. The sounds of battle had stopped. The air was as still as on any winter morning in the years before the enemy came.

Ling Tan went to the kitchen to find Ling Sao. 'This is the day we have feared,' he said.                                                      5

'I know it,' she said, quietly.

When all had eaten Ling Tan spoke to them as the head of the house. 'It is quiet out there and I know that the battle is over. Our army has retreated. But we must all stay within the      10
walls of our own house. None of you is to go out without telling me, and especially no woman is to show her face for any cause.'

The long silent day began. The women set to work in the house, Wu Lien went to his room and the sons sat and made     15
straw sandals. Ling Tan sat and smoked his pipe. Every family in the village did the same.

In a few hours Ling Tan went out of his gate and looked towards the city but the road was empty and there was no sign of anyone on it. Others opened their gates and did the      20
same and soon the men stood in the street speaking to each other.

'Have you heard any news?' Ling Tan asked.

'None,' they all answered.

Then one young man said, 'I will go to the city. I am not    25
afraid.'

'Go and ask your father for permission,' Ling Tan told the wilful* young man.

'I need no permission,' he said quickly and he walked off towards the city, fearless in his youth.                                           30

'I'm glad he is not my son,' said one of the men, and the others agreed.

There was nothing else to say, so the men parted and each man went back to his own house and locked his gate again.

*wilful*, acting with determination; not caring about the opinion of others.

41

The silence continued but by mid-afternoon the people were weary of hiding in their homes. A few children and parents began to go out into their courtyards to get some fresh air, and Ling Tan and his family did the same. Still, there was no
5   sign of the enemy and the afternoon passed and the people were relieved that the day was almost over.

Soon it was time for supper and it was twilight when Ling Tan next looked out of his gate. He and the family had eaten a good meal and all but he and Ling Sao were sleeping.
10  When he looked out of the gate he thought he heard a moan. He listened and then he knew it was the moan of a man. He threw the gate open and shouted for Ling Sao to bring the lamp. There, on the ground, lay his cousin's son, the young man who had gone to the city that morning.
15  'Oh, he is bleeding!' Ling Sao cried.

'Do not touch him, I will go and get his parents,' said Ling Tan. He ran down the shadowy street to find the boy's parents.

'Oh, my son is wounded and bleeding!' cried his mother.
20  The men looked at the boy and saw the wound in his chest.

'We must move him to a bed,' Ling Tan said. He and the other men carried the boy to a bed in his father's house.

'The enemy,' said the boy in the faintest voice, 'kill you if
25  you run.' Then he fell into a coma* and spoke no more.

The men heard what he had said and they looked at each other, all thinking the same thoughts. 'Why would the enemy kill innocent, unarmed people?' But no one dared to speak it aloud.
30  Ling Tan returned to his own home. It was the middle of the night and he sat until the dawn, smoking his pipe. Then, he heard the noise they had all feared for months.

---

*coma, a deep sleep; loss of consciousness.

42

*The enemy*

It was a grey morning, and when Ling Tan looked out of the gate it seemed that the grey was moving towards the village. He looked again. He did not know what it was exactly, but he knew this "grey" was the enemy.

He ran back to the house and gasped, 'The enemy is    5
coming. Everyone, get up and get ready for what will happen.'

Then he ran out and yelled for the other men of the village to join him. He told the innkeeper to prepare the tea and cakes and set them out on tables. The men gathered together   10
to walk down the road and greet the enemy.

Through the mist they could see only the strange, huge, grey shapes. Slowly they walked towards them, carrying the paper flags. But the strange shapes bore down on them as though they were ants and to save themselves they had to   15
step aside and let them pass. Now Ling Tan and the others saw that these shapes were machines, and how could they speak a welcome to machines. They stood staring as the shapes passed through the village and continued on.

They asked each other, 'Is this the enemy?' But none had   20
the answer.

They waited a while longer, then they heard the sound of tramping feet and saw the dim shapes of walking men. And these they knew were the real enemy.

Gathered together they stood in the road, waiting. When   25
the leaders of the enemy drew near they bowed and an old man began to speak a few words of welcome.

But the others knew that the faces of the enemy were not good. They were fierce and savage faces with unnatural smiles.   30

Ling Tan spoke. 'Sirs, we are only farmers and we are men of peace and reason and we welcome law and order. We have no weapons, but we have prepared a few cakes and tea— '

One of the enemy shouted, 'Where is your inn?'   35

'In the middle of our village street,' said Ling Tan, and

43

he was pleased that at least one of the enemy spoke their language, however poorly. At least they could be understood.

'Lead us there,' said the enemy man who spoke their language.

5 Ling Tan was frightened because he knew the faces of men, and these men looked at him and his neighbours with hate and disrespect. But they had no choice and the little band of villagers led the enemy to the tea-house.

They sat down at the tables and looked at the pots of 10 tea. The enemy man shouted, 'Wine — we want wine!'

'Alas, sir, we have no wine,' said Ling Tan, shakily.

The enemy man told the others this news. Then he shouted, 'Women! What women do you have in this village?'

Now Ling Tan could not believe what he had heard. 15 'Women?' His heart pounded and he quickly said, 'We will go and find women for you.' And he and all the others ran out of that back gate towards their homes as quickly as their terror would carry them.

Ling Tan shut his gate behind him and drew a bar across 20 it. He called the family together and as he started to speak to them he heard the enemy pounding on his gate. He knew it would not hold for very long.

'Every one of you is to go to that little back gate that has been locked for many years. Go out from that gate and 25 scatter yourselves over the land and hide in the bamboos,' he shouted.

'I will stay with you,' said Ling Sao and Ling Tan knew she would.

He took the family out the back to the little gate and at 30 once they all knew that Wu Lien's fat mother would not fit through the narrow passage. He pushed the others through, then turned to the sobbing old woman and took her to the corner of the garden and hid her behind some vines.

'Stop your crying and stand here, quietly,' he commanded 35 her.

*Death!*

He took Ling Sao and went back into the main room of the house. He climbed on the table and swung up to the big beam above it. Ling Sao followed him, like an old cat. They reached the roof and went into the thick thatch and covered themselves, almost choking in the straw and dust.                    5

Just as they had settled themselves into their hiding place, they heard the gate crash and the noise of angry men's voices. Ling Sao clung to Ling Tan and they hid, frozen with fear.

The men below them saw that the room was empty    10
and they screamed and ran from one room in the house to another. Ling Tan and Ling Sao heard the crash of their good china, and the breaking of furniture, but they did not care as they only wanted to remain hidden and alive.

Then they heard a scream. The enemy had found Wu    15
Lien's old mother. They heard a word or two, a gurgle*
and then silence. They both knew that the old woman was dead.

Long after there was silence Ling Tan and his wife dared not move or speak. In a while they looked at each other and    20
decided to go down. Ling Tan went first and saw that the enemy was gone. He helped Ling Sao down the beam and they stood in the main room of the house.

Destruction lay all around them. There was nothing left whole and the house was in ruin. Yet they knew the worst    25
was waiting for them in the garden.

They crept through the door to the small back court*.
The old woman lay dead at their feet. It would have been enough had she just been dead. But she was worse than dead.
She was naked, and they saw that these men had used her    30
body as they might have used a woman who was young and beautiful.

Ling Tan cried out and turned to his wife. 'If this enemy

---

*gurgle*, sound of bubbles in the throat.   *back court*, space behind a house surrounded by a wall or buildings.

45

is evil enough to do this to an old woman, they would do it to you. I must find a place to hide you, my wife.' He felt sick at the sight on the ground before him.

They could not lift the huge body of the old woman so
5 they covered her and went and sat in their kitchen. All the rest of the day they sat in the ruined house, waiting for night. By nightfall the eldest and youngest son came home.

'Father, we took the women and children to a safe place in the city,' whispered Lao Ta.
10 'The city! What place can be safe in the city?' he cried.

'It is the foreign school, father. There is a good and kind foreign woman there and she is taking the children and the women inside her gate. And the enemy dare not touch the foreigners,' he explained to his bewildered* father.
15 'Then, your mother must go. Now!' he shouted at the eldest.

Ling Sao knew Ling Tan meant this command and she prepared to leave him. The sons turned their backs while Ling Tan and Ling Sao parted from one another for the first
20 time in their married life. They held each other close and spoke the words of love. Then Ling Sao left with Lao Ta.

'Sleep, my father,' said Lao San after they left.

'No, I will await his safe return,' he said. He sat in the ruins of his house and waited. After a long time, Lao Ta returned.
25 'I put her through the gate, myself,' he said. 'She is safe.'

Ling Tan sighed, and his sons soon fell asleep. But he could not sleep for all that he had seen that day kept him wide awake.

*bewildered, confused.

# 7
## The White Woman and her House

Ling Sao looked at the white woman in the dimness\*. The
gate shut behind her and her son was gone. She was locked
in this strange place with this strange woman. The woman
had hair as yellow as cat's fur and even her eyes looked a
pale yellow to Ling Sao.

'Come with me and I will show you where your daughters
are,' said the woman. Ling Sao was frightened that she could
understand her speech.

'Is this magic that I can understand you?' she said to the
woman.

The white woman laughed a small laugh. 'I have spent
twenty years in this city,' she said, 'and I study every day to
speak your language, so that I may tell you of the one true
religion. Why is it so strange that you understand me?'

She led Ling Sao along a narrow brick wall and they came
to a great house. Ling Sao had never before seen a place such
as this. The woman led her into this house and it was full of
people.

'Your daughters and their children are in that corner,' said
the woman.

She moved to that side of the room and she found Orchid
and her two daughters and the children. Pansiao was lying
awake and when she saw her mother she sat up and put out
both her arms crying, 'Mother!'

'Yes, I am here, meat dumpling,' Ling Sao answered. She
sat and cradled Pansiao in her arms.

'Where is father?' cried Pansiao.

'He is at home with your two brothers,' she answered.

'Mother, they are good people here,' said Pansiao. 'They
fed us.'

\*_dimness_, almost darkness.

47

Ling Sao was confused as to what kind of place this was but for now she held her daughter and was content that they were all alive.

The elder daughter lifted up her head and said, 'Where is
5  Wu Lien's mother?'

Ling Sao knew that her daughter had a right to ask this question but she could not bear to tell her the truth. So she lied. 'She is so old that she is safe at home. Where is your husband?'

10  'Wu Lien led us here then he said he was going back to the shop. He is not afraid now that the city has fallen, for he said that the next thing is peace. When all is settled he will come

and take us home. Perhaps that will be sooner than we think.'

Ling Sao looked around the space where she and her family were. Women and children lined the room, lying or sitting on bamboo mats.

Soon her family fell asleep again but Ling Sao could not sleep. She sat up through the night thinking of what she had seen that day.

When the sun was well up there were serving women who brought rice and some salt fish in great buckets, chopsticks and bowls for everyone.

Ling Sao cried out, 'How can we eat when we have no money to pay for it?'

The women who carried the buckets laughed and told her to eat. 'Eat, good mother,' they said.

'Is this why she came here? To help us?' she said, wondering what this was all about. But the women had no time to answer for there were many mouths to feed and they moved along the room.

### The enemy

So began this strange day in Ling Sao's life. The great house was full of a hundred or more women, not counting the children. After they ate, the women went out to the grounds of the house and they knew they could walk freely on the green grass for the house was surrounded by a huge wall that few men could get over. The women spoke to each other, telling what they had seen of this terrible enemy, that came in madness and destroyed all it could.

Some of the women cried and told the tales of seeing their children killed before their eyes and all stood in a daze of horror at the thoughts of an enemy so cruel. They spoke of men killed, unarmed men killed, as they ran from the enemy troops. The women talked and cried and mourned through the day and into the evening.

When night came Ling Sao was exhausted and filled with a fear she had never known before. 'Beasts, they are like animals or worse,' she thought.

Deep in the middle of that night she woke, as did all those in the house. They heard thundering against the gates and the shots of guns. Soon they heard loud voices. They were the voices of men speaking a language they did not understand.

In a few minutes the white woman appeared in the hall and said, 'I have bad news; the enemy is at the gate. There are a hundred armed men there. They say they will come in and I have no power to keep them out. I have no arms, and I have only the power of my God and my country to hold them back. They do not fear my God, but they do fear my country a little. My country is a great nation. Because of this they have not yet come in, and so I have been able to buy them with a price.'

She looked over the faces in the room and her voice shook with her next words.                                                                5

'They say they will not come in if we give them a few women who will go away with them, perhaps five or six, even —'

She was then silent, and all of them were silent. None could speak.                                                                          10

The white woman waited and the noise at the gate began again.

'I cannot hold them back,' she cried. 'They say they will come in if I don't give them a few women. Oh, my sisters!'

Then Ling Sao saw that which she was never to forget so       15
long as she lived. A thing that she kept in her heart towards all women called "evil" by proper women.

'Come, we must go to work,' said the voice of a courtesan* who had taken refuge in this house.

The beautiful young girls stood before the white woman        20
and said, 'We are ready.'

'God give you his blessing and take you to Heaven for this,' the white woman cried.

But one of the beautiful little courtesans shook her head and said, 'Your God does not know us.' Then she and her       25
fellow courtesans went through the great house to the front gate and the waiting enemy.

There was no more noise at the gate and the night passed and the dawn came. The women were silent, their hearts full for what the courtesans had done for the rest of them. They       30
fed their children and spent a quiet day. Each was filled with her own thoughts.

The white woman did not come to see them that day, and then the night fell again.

*courtesan, prostitute, especially one whose customers are wealthy or important men.

51

# 8
## The East Ocean Enemy

Wu Lien worked in his shop alone. For the first three days he did not go out into the street, but he did do one important thing: he took soot from the kitchen chimney and mixed it with water and he wrote large black letters on the outside of
5  his shop. The letters said, "East Ocean Goods Sold Here".

It was not too long after he had put up his sign that four enemy soldiers came by to see if he had any food to sell. The men wanted salted fish, but all that Wu Lien had was some small fish soaked in oil and stored in tin boxes.

10  'How much?' the officer asked.

Wu Lien was surprised. 'Nothing — it is a gift.'

The officer stared at him, then smiled. 'You do not hate us?'

'I hate no one,' he answered.

15  The officer bowed, took the tins of fish and sat down on a small stool by the counter. 'We are sorry for the destruction we have inflicted* on your city.'

'I know how war and soldiers are. Let us now hope for peace,' Wu Lien said, smiling.

20  The officer told Wu Lien to fetch him paper and pen. Then he wrote some bold black letters that Wu Lien could not read and he gave the paper to Wu Lien.

'If anyone comes here to give you trouble, show them that paper,' he said.

25  'Oh, how can I thank you?' cried Wu Lien.

'I will send you a sign from our headquarters to put in front of your door and a guard if that is not enough.'

'Oh, thank you again and again, but I need no guard. Just the sign,' said Wu Lien, not wanting a guard in his shop.

30  'We are pleased with you, merchant. Tell everyone we will

*inflicted, put by force.

52

do no harm to those who do not resist us.'

The soldiers bid Wu Lien good day, and left his shop. He sat down and wiped his forehead for his whole body was streaming with sweat. 'They aren't so bad,' he thought. 'If I don't resist, my family and my business will prosper again.'     *5*

He slept fairly well that night and made plans to find his new friends, the soldiers, the next day and ask them if it was safe for his wife and family to move from the white lady's home to their own.

## Ling Tan and the enemy

In his own house Ling Tan and his sons made a coffin for     *10* Wu Lien's mother. They built the coffin and then with ropes and poles they lifted that great body and heaved* it into the coffin and nailed the lid shut. With the buffalo pulling on ropes and all of them pushing, they dragged the coffin into the fields and buried Wu Sao.     *15*

Then they went back into their house and they began to sort out the ruins and mend what they could, so that they could live. The others in the community did the same to their homes. They worked for a few days with no sign of any return of the enemy.     *20*

Then the enemy began to come from the city and go into the villages. One day Ling Tan looked up and there at his door stood four enemy soldiers. He put down his basket and went to the door for he knew there was no use in pretending they were not there. He threw the door open. They     *25* shouted at him and at first he thought they wanted food, for he could not understand their language. Then they pointed at themselves and he saw they wanted women and they demanded his women.

'There are no women in my house,' he said, shaking his     *30* head.

But they could not understand him, either. They leaped

---

*heaved*, lifted something heavy with difficulty.

53

in and pushed him aside, searching every room for themselves. They saw for themselves that there were no women and they became very angry.

5 Their lust* burst from them when they saw the youngest son, Lao San, who had always been too beautiful for his own good. They layed hold upon this boy and used him as a woman. Ling Tan and Lao Ta could not bear this and they jumped on the wicked soldiers. The soldiers tied them up and made them watch what they did with Lao San. Then,
10 those soldiers went on their way, laughing.

Ling Tan and his sons said not a word. Slowly, he and Lao Ta untied themselves. Ling Tan took some water and washed his youngest son and put clothes on him and tried to comfort the boy. But he was like a dead one; as though his heart had
15 been stabbed and his father was afraid he had gone mad.

'My little son,' he said, 'you are alive.'

'I wish I were dead,' the boy whispered. His beautiful black eyes were like eyes of the dead. 'I cannot stay here.'

'I know,' said Ling Tan. 'You must go to the hills and hide
20 your beautiful face.' He prepared some food for the boy to carry with him.

Slowly, Lao San rose and put on his heavy sandals. He and Ling Tan went to the front gate and saw that the street was deserted.

25 'Send me word of where you are, somehow' said Ling Tan sadly.

'I will, father,' cried the boy. He held fast to his father for a few minutes. Then he left his home and headed for the hills.

30 Ling Tan and Lao Ta stood and watched him until they could no longer see the figure in the dark of night. 'Is there anything else that can happen to us?' cried Ling Tan to his eldest son. His son did not answer and together they went back into their ruined home. Lao Ta barred* the door.

35 'Can you eat if I cook the rice?' he asked his father.

---

*lust, a strong desire. *barred, fastened by putting a bar across.

'I feel tonight as if I could never eat again,' Ling Tan answered.

'I feel the same,' said Lao Ta.

Each man went into his own room, but after a while Ling Tan got up and went into his son's room.                    5

'I cannot close my eyes without seeing again in my mind the horror we saw tonight,' he said.

'Stay in here with me father,' said Lao Ta.

There they lay, two men left alone in this house that had been so full, and they did not speak for each knew what    10
the other was thinking. They did not sleep. Together their minds followed the slender figure of the boy, limping alone, through the night towards the hills.

# 9
## Wu Lien and the Enemy

For a day or two Wu Lien thought about his situation. He made up his mind one night that he would find the officer who had been courteous to him and tell him all his troubles.

He waited until night came and then, putting on his oldest 5 clothes, he went to the street which the officer had written on the paper he had left with him. He knocked on a closed door. After some time the door was opened by a soldier and Wu Lien's knees knocked together with fear because the soldier's face was so angry. He held out the paper, and after 10 looking at it for a while the soldier pulled him inside the door and told him to follow him through the house.

Wu Lien went into the house behind him. There in the main room were three or four enemy officers drinking together. The officer Wu Lien knew looked up at him with 15 cold eyes, and Wu Lien suddenly wished he had not come to this place at all.

'Sir, I come here on business and I am sorry that I have disturbed your good time,' Wu Lien said in a shaky voice.

'Speak, then,' the officer said, coldly.

20 'I am a citizen of this city and I have the shop that you saw and I have long dealt with foreign goods. For the most part my foreign goods come from your honourable country. I desire nothing but peace so that I may go on with my business. Whoever is to rule, let him rule. I do not care so long 25 as I can trade. There are those in this city who call me a traitor and wish to kill me because I have dealt with your honourable country in trade. So, I come to you, who now rule, and ask if there is any way that I can be made safe.' Wu Lien waited fearfully for the reply.

30 The officer who understood what Wu Lien had said translated it for the others. Then they talked together for a while before answering him.

'You may be useful to us, if you wish,' said the officer.

'Yes, sir, tell me.'

'We shall set up a people's government here, and it will be a government of those who will rule for us. What is your ability?' the officer asked.                                                    5

'I am skilled at the abacus. I can read and write—'

'Do you know English?' said the officer, cutting him short.

'Alas, I do not,' Wu Lien answered, sadly.

'But you say you can write?'                                             10

'Yes,' he answered. Then he waited while they spoke together.

'You will move into this house at once. You will have a title and you will be paid according to your abilities. Come here tomorrow.'                                                       15

When he heard this Wu Lien's head began to whirl*. 'But, kind sir, I have a wife, my old mother and two children,' he said.

'They may all come here,' said the officer. 'They will be safe here and you also. Rooms will be given to them.'       20

Wu Lien was happy and praised the gods for his good fortune. 'May I bring my few things here at once?' he asked.

'Yes, you may come at once if you wish,' answered the officer. 'You see how merciful we are to those who do not resist us?'                                                           25

'Yes, great one,' agreed Wu Lien, bowing three times. He put his goods together when he returned to his shop that night. He found a rickshaw, packed it and made his way to the enemy house. The next day he put on his best clothes and, with a guard of two enemy soldiers, went to       30 the white woman's house.

*Wu Lien collects his family*

He beat on the gate. A little window opened and the gate-

*to whirl, to spin.

57

man looked out at Wu Lien and the soldiers.

'I am Wu Lien and I have come for my family,' he said in the confident voice of an official.

'I cannot let those soldiers in here,' the gateman said.

5   Wu Lien understood. 'I will come in and get my household.'

But the gateman was afraid and did not understand why Wu Lien, one of his own people, was with the enemy. He went and got the white woman.

10   The white woman looked out through the window in the gate. She said to Wu Lien, 'Are you a traitor?'

Wu Lien was angry. 'Woman, I want my family. They will be safe with me.'

'Have you not seen what these men, your friends, have
15   done to the people of the city?' she asked angrily.

'That is finished and now there will be peace,' he said.

She looked at Wu Lien with distaste and opened the gate. 'You wait here and I will bring your family to you,' she said, coldly.

20   In a few minutes Wu Lien's wife, family and Ling Sao came running to him.

Ling Sao was surprised to see him with the soldiers and she remembered that Wu Lien did not know that his own mother was dead. 'Son-in-law, I have some bad news for you,' she
25   said, but she could not bear to tell him the truth of what had happened to her at the hands of the evil enemy. 'Your mother is dead, she was crushed under a beam and my husband buried her.'

Wu Lien wept for his mother but the soldiers were im-
30   patient and they prodded him with the butts* of their rifles.

'Wife, you are coming with me,' he said quickly.

'Is my daughter safe with you?' cried Ling Sao.

'Yes, I am protected and so are all who belong to me.' Then he grabbed his family and left Ling Sao standing at
35   the gate with the white woman.

*butts, the thick ends of guns.

58

'I am sorry for you, poor woman,' said the white lady, and she walked away.

Ling Sao did not understand why the white woman said these words to her. 'Why does she pity me when there are others who have suffered much more?' she asked the gateman.

'Because,' the gateman said, 'your daughter's husband has gone over to be a running dog of the enemy.'

Ling Sao thought of this as she walked back into the hall where Orchid was. She told everything to Pansaio and Orchid, and the more they talked together the more these women wanted to be free.

Soon the story went through the entire hall and there was restlessness when the women heard that one of them had gone home. 'Things must be better,' each woman thought to herself. And Ling Sao spoke to Orchid and Pansiao, saying, 'It is still not safe out there. How I wish I could go to my home too.'

It was late and Ling Sao and Pansiao lay down for a rest before their dinner. But Orchid did not sleep. She smiled at Ling Sao and Pansiao and was very quiet. And, worst of all, she did not believe Ling Sao's words. 'It must be safe,' she thought, 'or why else would Wu Lien come and take them away to their home.'

## Death

Orchid did not sleep well that night. She thought of her lucky sister-in-law and how she was out of this place. The next day a letter came from the eldest daughter, telling of her happiness and good fortune. This made Orchid more restless.

'The city is at peace again and there is no reason why I cannot steal out of the gate some morning and see what there is in the shops. I might even go to visit my sister-in-law, and then, if all seems well I will send word to my husband, and we can go home, again.' These words she dared not say out loud, she only thought them to herself.

The next day when all in her family were busy with chores*
in the hall, she quietly left them and went to the front gate.
She waited until the gateman went inside his little house to
eat his meal. Then she drew the bar on the gate softly so that
5  he would not hear. She slipped through the gate and went
happily down the street, feeling like a bird set free.

She did not know it but she was being watched by the
enemy as she went down that street. As she passed a public
water-closet* for men, five enemy soldiers grabbed her and
10  drew her inside.

When they had her inside, they held her fast and used her
for their pleasure.
She screamed and they beat her, one holding his hand over
her nose and mouth. She struggled and then the life went out
15  of her and she died.

An hour later a passer-by used the water-closet and found
the dead Orchid. 'I will take her to the white woman,' he
said. He called a rickshaw and he and the driver pulled the
body to the gate.
20  The gateman, recognized Orchid and realizing what must
have happened, ran to get the white woman.

The white woman came and with others helping they
carried the body to the temple hall and laid it on a table.
Then she went to find Ling Sao.
25  At first Ling Sao thought the white woman had made a
mistake. But she followed her to the temple and saw Orchid's
body. She cried out, 'But I saw her three hours ago. Alive.'

The white woman comforted her.

'Oh,' Ling Sao cried. 'I don't know what to do. Send for
30  my husband and my son, please.'

'I have already done so,' said the woman.

Ling Sao returned to the hall and told some of the women
what had happened. Then she sat, weeping and waiting for
Ling Tan and Lao Ta.
35  It was late that evening when the gateman came and told

*chores, jobs. *water-closet, lavatory.

her to come to the front gate with him. She followed him and  when she saw her husband and her son she wept and wept.

The white woman had already met the men and told them what had happened. Ling Tan put his arms around his wife.  5

'Follow me,' said the white woman. They followed her into a room where she prayed and read from a black book. 'I will find a coffin for Orchid and for the time being you can bury her here. When times are better you may take her and bury her on your land.'  10

Ling Tan spoke for the others. 'Your mercy is beyond our understanding. Thank you.'

'Do not thank *me*, I do it in the name of God.'

They did not understand this so they did not answer.

'Husband, I am going home with you,' Ling Sao said.  15

Now, Ling Tan knew his woman and he knew she was coming with him no matter what he said.

'What of Panisao? Will you leave her here, alone?' he asked.

The white woman answered before Ling Sao could speak. 'Leave your daughter with me. We had a girls' school here in  20 the good times, but we have moved the school a thousand miles up the river. One of our ships comes tomorrow to take some of the others to the school. She can go with them and she will be safe. When you want her back, I will send for her.'

Ling Tan spoke for the family, again. 'We will trust you.'  25

'Good. Your daughter will learn to read and write at our school,' said the woman.

Then, Lao Ta spoke. 'I want to see my wife.'

The white woman took them to the temple hall. Ling Sao was grateful when she saw that the white woman had bathed  30 and dressed the body.

Lao Ta looked at the sleeping face of his wife. He could not believe she was dead. The tears came up his throat and welled* into his eyes and ran down his cheeks. He turned to the white woman and said, 'Cover her.'  35

*welled*, sprang up.

61

They went out of the hall and Ling Tan and Lao Ta waited while Ling Sao dressed the children and told Pansiao the news.

'The woman says you will learn to read and write,' said
5 Ling Sao.

Pansiao's heart leapt in her chest for this was what she wanted more than anything in the whole world. But she dared not show this to her mother so she was quiet. She went with her mother to the front gate.

10 'Don't be afraid and write us a letter when you learn how,' Ling Tan said to his daughter.

'Yes, father,' she said, quietly.

Then Ling Tan, Ling Sao, Lao Ta and his children thanked the white woman for her kindness and said farewell to
15 Pansiao. They went out of the gate quietly.

'Come with me, child,' said the white woman to Pansiao. 'Can you be happy with us?'

And she saw the young girl's face full of joy and heard her say, 'I can be very happy with you.'

*Ling Sao returns home*
20 Late that night Ling Tan and his family arrived home safely. But Ling Sao wept bitterly when she saw her ruined home. 'Where is our youngest son?' she asked, expecting him to greet her.

Ling Tan told her the truth of the horror that had hap-
25 pened to their beautiful boy, and she wept some more. But there was an envelope waiting for them on the table and absent-mindedly, Ling Tan opened it. He shouted for joy in the midst of his pain.

'What do you smile about?' his wife asked, tearfully.
30 He held up a braided cord of red silk and a letter. 'I cannot read the letter but the cord is from Jade and our son. Mother of my children, we have a new grandson!'

## 10

## *Letters*

In the midst of all their trouble here was their joy. The next day as soon as they had washed and eaten they went to their cousin's house. Ling Tan asked him to read the letter.

The cousin prepared himself for the reading in true scholarly fashion, washing his face and hands and rinsing his mouth. He cleared his throat and began the letter.                    5

It read, 'Our father and mother. We hope you are well and that all is safe with you and our elder brother. Give him our wishes.' With this Ling Sao wept but the cousin read on. 'Since we left our good home we have travelled well     10
over a thousand miles and now we are here as we have paused for the birth of our child. We dare not stay long for there are rumours that the enemy is coming here, too.

Your grandson was born on the last day of the thirteenth month, a little before his time because Jade had walked so    15
far. The child is well and strong. When times are good we will return with him and show him to you. If times are still bad we will then go on to the upper reaches of the river and from there I will write again. If you send us a letter, send it to a man named Liu, the owner of the shop on the corner of Fish      20
Market Street and Needle Street. Please write to us and tell of the family news. Farewell, Lao Er and family.' Thus the letter ended.

Now that the letter was over, Ling Tan and Ling Sao smelled the stench of their cousin's son, the one wounded     25
the day the enemy came.

'How is he?' Ling Tan asked, pleasantly.

'The maggots* are in his stomach, now. He will be dead today or tomorrow,' said his cousin's wife, tearfully.

They went and looked at the boy and they saw the       30

*maggots*, kind of worms which eat flesh.

maggots on his wound and they knew he was not long for this world. They thanked their cousin and quietly left the house. The boy died one hour later.

*Life goes on*

5 When they arrived home, Ling Tan and Ling Sao spoke of Lao Er's letter. 'You must ask our cousin to write a letter and tell Lao Er and Jade and the baby to return. You and Lao Ta have too much work for both of you. We need them here with us,' said Ling Sao.

'Let me think about it,' Ling Tan said. He was not sure if 10 it was the right or safe thing to do.

Ling Tan and Lao Ta went back to the fields. Day after day they ploughed back and forth in silence. Ling Tan would look over at the widowed Lao Ta, and think, 'There is one whose life has been ruined by this war.' And he felt the anger 15 inside himself boil and he ploughed faster to rid* himself of it.

It was a joyless spring. One festival followed another and Ling Sao made no feasts, nor did any other of the women in the village. Ling Tan's house was silent and there was no joy.

20 The days passed in that spring but the summer brought more tragedy for Ling Tan and the village people. The new disaster was worse than the laws the enemy made about the price of rice.

In the past year so many people had died that it was im- 25 possible to bury them all. Those that could not be buried were thrown into the canals and rivers and when the river rose up that spring, sickness came to those left alive. The heat of the summer brought fever which spread everywhere.

It fell upon Ling Tan's house and took the youngest and 30 weakest. The whole family was ill for ten days and Lao Ta's two little children died.

Ling Sao wept as she never had before and Ling Tan's

*to rid, to make oneself free of something.

64

spirit was so low he could not speak. Lao Ta could not bear any more pain and so he spoke to his father. 'I want to go away for a while,' he said in a dull voice.

'But where will you go?' cried Ling Sao.

'I do not know, but I must go away,' he said.                          *5*

Ling Tan knew his son was fast losing his will* to live and he had an idea. 'Son, go and find Lao San and tell us if he is well.'

Lao Ta opened his eyes a little wider and said, 'Is that a command, father?'                                                       *10*

'Yes,' said his father.

'I will do it,' he answered, purposefully.

And though Ling Tan was sad to see another son leave the land, he knew he had given Lao Ta a reason to live.

Lao Ta left that evening. Within an hour, Ling Sao said to      *15* Ling Tan, 'Now, you must write to Lao Er and Jade for you cannot do the work yourself.'

'Tomorrow I will send a letter to our second son,' said Ling Tan, and Ling Sao was happy.

The next day Ling Tan sat in his cousin's house telling him     *20* what to write to his son. 'Tell my son that he must understand he does not come back to peace, for there can be no peace. Tell him that I and his mother are alone, that my other sons have gone to the hills, that my eldest son's wife and children are dead. Tell him Pansiao has gone with the     *25* white woman. Tell him I will hold the land as long as I can. And lastly, tell him he is not to come if it is too dangerous.'

His cousin wrote the letter for him and within a few days they found a messenger who would carry the letter for a fee. They paid him and put the letter in his trust.                     *30*

Ling Tan was worried about Jade. 'Where will we hide her when she comes back?' he asked Ling Sao. For they both knew what the enemy would do to Jade if they found her.

Ling Sao thought about this problem for one whole day. That night when Ling Tan returned from his work in the       *35*

*will, desire.

65

fields she spoke to him of her idea.

'We will dig a hole through the earthen floor of the kitchen behind the stove and then under the earthen wall of the house under the courtyard. Then we could cover the hole
5 with a board and put straw on it.'

Ling Tan looked at his wife and smiled, 'You are a clever woman.' And they went to work on her idea at once, planning the digging.

The next night the two began to dig their hole and con-
10 tinued adding a few inches to the hole every day. This helped to pass the time while they waited for their son and Jade and the new grandchild to arrive.

## Ling Tan talks to the enemy

One day, to Ling Tan's terror, he saw a band of the enemy coming towards him in his field. He stood, waiting to die, but
15 he saw that they did not take out their swords or draw their guns. They had come to talk to him.

One of the enemy had a little book and he spoke Ling Tan's language. He asked him questions; what was his name, how much land did he have and how much rice would he
20 have from the planted crop. Ling Tan was used to tax-gatherers so he told them he would have far less crop than he really would and then he was silent.

They asked him more questions and he answered them by saying that he had one water-buffalo, two pigs, eight chick-
25 ens, a pond with some fish and ducks and that in his house there only lived himself and his old wife. 'We are childless,' he lied.

The little man wrote this down and then he said one more thing to Ling Tan, 'Beginning with the first of the month
30 there is to be control of all fish, and only we shall eat fish. You farmer, if you catch any fish in your ponds you must not eat them. Bring them to us.'

'But the pond is mine,' said Ling Tan, for fish was their chief meat.

'Nothing is yours!' bellowed* the man. 'You are conquered* and you will do exactly as we say!' Then the enemy left him.

When the enemy was out of sight he ran all the way back to the village. He saw his neighbours too. They all met in the street and spoke of the new laws the evil enemy had imposed on them. He went home and told Ling Sao what the enemy had said.

'Go and buy as much salt as you can,' she said simply.

'But why?' he asked.

'Because we are not going to give them anything! Those pigs must die, and half the chickens and we will eat salt fish.'

Ling Tan saw the wisdom in her words and he went and bought the salt. Late that night they killed, dried and salted their fowls and their pigs.

From that night onwards, whenever they saw the enemy coming, Ling Sao would hide the salted meat and fish in the hole behind the stove.

The summer was long that year while Ling Tan and Ling Sao waited for their son and grandson. But there was the hole to dig.

At last one night, the hour came for which they had waited. There was a knocking on the gate and at first Ling Tan thought it was the enemy. But he heard the words he had waited for.

'Father! Father!'

He threw open the gate and pulled in Lao Er and Jade. They went to the kitchen and found their mother. 'Where is the baby?' she demanded.

And Jade opened her loose coat and handed Ling Sao a beautiful grandson. The boy looked at his grandmother and smiled. Ling Sao and Ling Tan wept openly for they were truly happy for the first time in many months.

*bellowed*, shouted angrily. *conquered*, overcome by force.

67

# Resistance*

Ling Tan and the family talked all through the night. Jade and Lao Er told of their journey and of the birth of their son. Ling Tan showed them the hole in the floor and Lao Er was very pleased. 'I will begin work on it tomorrow,' he said.

5　　The next day, in the fields, Ling Tan wondered whether or not he could keep his son's arrival a secret in the village. It seemed to him that he could, but should not hide anything from the village. 'After all,' he thought, 'they are my own blood.'

10　　So, that night after the day's work he took his son to the village tea-shop. When all in the shop turned and saw Ling Tan and Lao Er, Ling Tan called for their attention.

'This son of mine has seen many things which he will tell you of, if you are willing to listen.'

15　　The village people clapped their hands on the table and waited for Lao Er to clear his throat and begin his tale.

He told his village how he had travelled to a city a thousand miles away until his father's letter reached him, then he had turned back, and that everywhere people were of one
20　mind. All the people he saw were of one mind to resist the enemy.

'There are only two kinds of men who won't resist the enemy. Those who wish to make their own profit and the others who are weak and evil; the opium takers! These two
25　kinds of men are dangerous because they are spies! These men are traitors.'

'Yes!' the crowd of villagers cried.

'Uncles and cousins, we must join ourselves to those in the free land who make war on the enemy. How? By working in
30　secret with the nine thousand men in the hills. You may ask.

*resistance*, stopping the advance of the enemy.

"What does this mean?" It means that we must hide our rice and wheat harvests and give the enemy as little as we can. It means that as often as possible an enemy or two will suddenly die from unseen guns.'

'But we have no guns,' one man cried.                                          5

'I know where to get guns, and every man shall have his own,' said Lao Er.

The men cheered for this gave them hope of resistance. And Ling Tan was the proudest man in the crowd.

Thereafter the people in that village waited for Lao Er to   10
bring them guns. He waited until he had finished the room under the court and a few of the villagers helped him. The secret room was big with strong beams across its ceiling. When it was finished Lao Er turned to his father and said, 'Now we have a place to put our guns.' The next morning he   15
went towards the hills.


## The harvest

The enemy sent men to oversee the rice harvest and esti-mate what the yield would be when it was ripe and ready to cut. Ling Tan and the men took their commands in silence but they planned well.                                          20

They cut their grain quickly and even at night when the enemy could not be everywhere. They dug holes under their kitchens and hid the grain. When the enemy wondered why the yield was so low, Ling Tan and the men told them sadly of the thick stalks that yielded less grain than expected. The   25
enemy could not kill the farmers for this because they knew that if they did there would be no one to farm the land next year. So, the enemy took what the men of Ling village gave them and sold it for five times the amount that they had paid the farmers. This made the farmers angry but secretly they   30
smiled as they knew thay had fooled the "little devils".

They would fish with a man on the lookout and dry and salt the fish and hide it in their homes. Once in a while one of the farmers would carry a few fish to the city and turn them in to the enemy, just to keep the devils convinced that they followed their orders on fishing. They secretly smiled at each other.

These peaceful, honest men learned quickly how to be
5 dishonest. The resistance grew and grew by the day.

The autumn days went on until Ling Tan's fields were bare of grain and he had hidden enough to feed his house. One night, at midnight, he heard a particular knock on the door. He knew the knock and he threw open the door to greet Lao
10 Er happily.

## The boys return home

'Father,' said three voices. Lao Ta, Lao Er and Lao San were standing together with their arms full of rifles and hand-guns.

He greeted them and woke Ling Sao. She was so happy to
15 see her three sons that she wept openly in front of them.

Ling Tan led them all to the secret room. The boys unloaded the guns. Ling Sao cooked the food and with Jade and the baby, they sat as a family for the first time in many months and ate a meal together.

20 It was decided that Lao Er would stay and the other two would return to the hills for more guns. Ling Sao was un-happy with this but she knew they had to go. She bade* them a tearful farewell and saw them to the gate. That night she and Ling Tan slept more soundly than they had in months, for
25 they knew that right now their three sons were alive. And dur-ing war time, "right now" was all that mattered to any one.

A few days later, at about noon, there was a noise at the gate. Lao Er and Jade took their baby and went down the steps behind the stove to the secret room. Ling Sao had
30 followed her husband to the gate, saw that it was Wu Lien and her daughter and ran back to tell Lao Er and Jade this news.

*bade, told.

## Wu Lien and the enemy

'No, dearest mother, we will not come out and don't tell them we are here or anything about this room!' shouted Lao Er.

Ling Sao did not understand this but she did as he wished as he was her second son and she loved him dearly.

When Ling Tan opened the gate and saw Wu Lien and his household, he was shocked beyond words for a moment. His eyes had grown used to the miserable people, afraid and hungry and wounded and fleeing*. Now he saw Wu Lien at his gate, fatter than ever. His daughter stood behind her husband, fat and pregnant*. The two children were fat and dressed in red silk coats, and they had all come in rickshaws. But what alarmed Ling Tan was the sight of two enemy soldiers behind them all.

'You are welcome, Wu Lien, and your family. But I cannot let those two into my house!'

Wu Lien laughed and said, 'You need not fear, they are my guards.'

'I realise that but I will not have them in my house!' repeated Ling Tan, angrily.

Then he went and got two stools and a bench and gave the bench to the guards and he and Wu Lien sat on the stools.

'Why are you so fat?' Ling Tan asked.

'My business is good,' answered Wu Lien.

'How can your business be so good when no one else's is good?'

'You must know that what I do is for the good of my family,' said Wu Lien nervously.

'What do you do?' cried Ling Tan loudly.

Wu Lien laughed nervously and explained how he worked for the new government and that he was an offical and that two clerks ran the shop for him. He told them of his fine house on a fine street and his cash and his food.

All the while Ling Tan stared in horror at the fat Wu Lien.

*fleeing*, running away. *pregnant*, expecting a baby.

71

'And, I am controller of *all* goods coming from the East Ocean,' said Wu Lien proudly. He saw the look on his father-in-law's face.

'I can help you,' whispered Wu Lien.

5 'We do not need your help,' cried Ling Tan.

'Come now, I control everything that comes in; the rice, wheat, opium and salt.'

'Opium!' said Ling Tan.

Wu Lien turned red. He remembered suddenly how much

10 his wife's father hated opium and he had not meant to say it. Opium was being brought down from the North. The enemy scattered it everywhere and they were telling villagers to use it.

Ling Tan spat on the ground in anger.

15 Inside the house Ling Sao questioned her daughter.

'Where do you get all this meat and rice to eat?' she asked.

'Mother, my husband gets it.'

'How is he able when the rest of the people are starving. What right do you people have to be fat when your own are

20 thin and hungry?' she yelled at her daughter.

Her daughter started to cry, seeing her mother displeased.

'He is a good husband and he says that every man has his own way of resisting the enemy. And he hates them in his heart and that is what matters,' the daughter said through her

25 tears.

Ling Sao could not even look at her grandchildren with love, knowing they had grown fat while other children starved. She looked coldly at her daughter and waited for her to leave.

30 The daughter stood and went to join her husband. Silently, Ling Sao followed. She and Ling Tan waited for them to leave, nodding a farewell to the children.

Ling Tan barred the gate after they had gone and Ling Sao shouted down the hole in the kitchen and the others came

35 up. They talked a while of the visit and Lao Er was angry. He made up his mind to go to the city. There, he would be able to see for himself if things were indeed as Wu Lien

had told Ling Tan. Immediately he told Jade what he planned to do and she set about making him a beggar's garment as a disguise. She put red clay on his face and leg to make them appear wounded.

## The truth

A few days after Wu Lien's visit, Lao Er went into the city 5 pretending he was a beggar. Avoiding the main streets, he came and went and said little and saw much. What angered and grieved him was the sale of opium. It was everywhere. The streets were silent and the houses still in ruins. People looked sad and many looked as though they were moving in 10 another world. Lao Er knew it was the dream-world of opium.

He limped home that night and told of what he had seen and how the markets had no food in them and the city people were starving. But the enemy did not care, and instead of food they gave the city people cheap opium so they would 15 forget they were hungry.

Ling Tan listened to Lao Er and sighed. 'What is our refuge* from all this? We can hide from the flying ships and we can build our homes again, but what can be done if the people take opium and forget what the enemy has done 20 to them?' To Ling Tan this seemed the worst evil that the enemy had done.

*refuge*, a place to shelter from danger.

## 12
## *The Secret War*

Now a secret war is more difficult to wage* than an open war.
As the winter passed, Ling Tan had to keep his face dull
and his eyes empty. Yet, his mind had to be quick to spring
to every advantage. His sons, and those who came with them,
5  used the secret room as a fortress*. To the enemy, Ling Tan
seemed to be an old farmer who knew nothing and saw
nothing.

In the spring there seemed to be so many of the enemy
found dead that a great anger rose among the enemy rulers.
10  Guards were found shot upon the city wall, though the city
gates were locked at night. The wall was eighty feet high
so how could anyone climb it?

But Ling Tan's youngest son, and others like him, climbed
that wall on many occasions. He would pull himself up,
15  from crevice* to crevice and creep along the wall until he
came to an enemy guard, then shoot him. Then he climbed
down and went home and before dawn he was back in the
hills.

The enemy who came to the countryside in search of food
20  and goods found themselves surrounded by innocent, dull
villagers. Then suddenly these dull people brought out guns
and fell upon them and killed them.

There were strange weapons in the secret room under
Ling Tan's court: bright new guns with foreign letters written
25  on them and ancient weapons from the men in the hills. Ling
Tan had chosen a strange old gun for his weapon and he
could fire it four times on one magazine*.

In his village Ling Tan was the man chosen to give the sign

---

*to wage (war), to carry on a war. *fortress, a place of protection, somewhere
well defended. *crevice, narrow opening in a rock or wall. *magazine, space for
bullets in a gun.

of death to the enemy and he did this whenever the enemy came. Twice in the winter and once in the spring he gave the sign and each time they were able to kill all the enemy so that not once did any escape to give a bad report of the village.

The enemy rulers grew angrier month by month, for how could they rule the countryside if they could not go out in it? At last, in the middle of the summer, the enemy began to burn all those villages where they found men of the hills. Ling Tan's village was not burned, for the men of the hills hid in his secret room and the enemy did not find them.

The people began to change as they heard stories of innocent children burned alive in their houses in the middle of the night. Their anger grew.

### Changes

One day in the first month of that summer a band of the enemy came to Ling Tan's village looking for wood. They were a band of eight men and Ling Tan saw they only carried five guns. The villagers watched Ling Tan and he gave the death sign and they fell upon the men. They all died except one who happened to crawl to Ling Tan's house.

'Let me live,' he cried to Ling Tan.

But Ling Tan reached inside the man's own belt and took out a short knife and without waiting a moment more, he thrust it into the man's belly.

Ling Tan stood and looked down at the man and thought of how easily he had taken the man's life. 'I have changed so very much,' he thought.

He thought of the changes in his sons. The youngest son, beautiful Lao San, had changed most of all. His beauty had become a terrible, cold beauty. When he came home after a night climbing and killing, he laughed and told the others the details of his deeds.

Now Ling Tan saw before his eyes that this son had become the sort of man he feared and hated most; a man who loved to make war and found it his pleasure in life. The once quiet boy was now full of zest and the men in the hills knew it too and they taught him to become a master of ambush* and death.

5 Ling Tan's heart was heavy because he knew it was too late to change the boy back to the innocent young man he had been. For himself, Ling Tan decided that he would kill no more and that he would resist in a quiet way.

Lao Er was more like his father. He killed when he must 10 but never for pleasure. He laid schemes for others to carry out and in this scheming no woman could have helped him more than Jade did.

'We ought to use Wu Lien as a gate into the enemy's fortress,' she told Lao Er one day.

15 'Yes, that is a fine idea, Jade,' said Lao Er.

'But he doesn't know we are in this part of the country,' said Jade, and then she thought of how to use Wu Lien in secret.

But she was wrong and Wu Lien did know that she and 20 Lao Er were in the village for there was one who was an informer among the villagers.

### The informer

Ling Tan's cousin's wife was a very bitter and jealous woman. She had lost her only son, and her scholar husband had little money. She was especially jealous of the beautiful 25 Jade and her happy marriage to Lao Er, and the beautiful child.

This woman had seen Wu Lien come to Ling Tan's house, fat and red in the face. And so one day she took some fresh fish she had caught and went into the city to the house where 30 Wu Lien lived.

Wu Lien greeted her and called his wife to join them.

'Your brothers are well,' she told Wu Lien's wife. 'I saw

*ambush*, hiding and waiting for the enemy.

the second one not many days ago.'

'Is he here?' cried the girl.

'Oh, yes and Jade, too. And they have a fine baby boy. I have also seen your two other brothers and I see them when they come down from the hills,' said the woman, knowing      5
she should have said none of this but war changes people and makes them bitter.

Then she went on to tell of her own troubles and waited for Wu Lien to pay her in some way.

'Cousin, your husband is a scholar and can write a fine      10
hand. Perhaps I could find a small job for him in our new government?' said Wu Lien.

'Oh, thank you, sir,' cried the woman. And she left Wu Lien and her cousin quite pleased with herself.

As she walked homewards she planned to keep Wu Lien      15
informed of all the happenings in Ling Tan's house, except for the secret room. She wouldn't dare tell anyone, not even Wu Lien, about the secret room for surely the enemy would swoop down on the village and kill them all if they knew about the guns. But she would feed him some information in      20
return for food, or a job for her husband and no one would ever know.

Jade and Lao Er did not know it, but Wu Lien knew about them.

Soon Jade had come up with her plan for using Wu Lien      25
as a gate to the enemy. She told her plan to Lao Er and he approved of it.


### Jade's plan

Jade put on a wig of grey hair, smeared her face with dye and put a false hump on her back. Then she went into the city to Wu Lien's house and approached the kitchen door,      30
selling cabbages. The guards were happy to see the fresh food for sale and they sent her to the cook who was one of her own countrymen.

Jade spent an hour with that cook and when she left the

kitchen everything was arranged. She returned to the village, purchased what she needed and delivered it to the cook the next day.

'If this succeeds, I will do it over and over again,' she
5   thought as she waited for news from the city.

At last the news did leak back, and it came through the cousin's wife. She said she had seen Wu Lien on the street and that he was as thin as a rake* as he had almost died from eating a feast with the enemy. And, she said, many of
10  the enemy who had eaten that feast had died.

Jade was pleased and told no one but Ling Tan's family what she had done, so the cousin did not know Jade was the one who had planned the poisoning.

'A good way to rid ourselves of them,' said Lao Er. 'We
15  must do it again.' Then he held Jade close to him and spoke words of love to her.

Jade smiled at Lao Er. The secret was continued and there was very little the enemy could do about it at all.

---

*rake, long pole with fork on the end used for gardening.

## 13
# The Whole World

Wu Lien was writing what the enemy told him to write. When he had finished writing, the enemy would take the copy and print it out many times in large letters and paste the papers on the walls of houses and temples.

The enemy would pause at every letter and say, 'Have you   5
written what I have told you to write?'

'I have, sir,' Wu Lien answered each time.

He looked down at the message today. "Star of Salvation! The New Order of East Asia!" and the signature was always the same, "Great People's Association". All these words   10
were supposed to come from the "new government" in the city, but all knew they came from the enemy house.

When Wu Lien finished his daily task of the writing, he would bow to the enemy and go to his rooms. He was well paid for his labours and he saved this money for the future.   15

He had made a friend of one of the enemy and often, in the afternoon, he would go and visit this enemy in his room. This enemy was a scholar and a writer and he was sent to learn the language of Wu Lien's country. It was in this man's room that Wu Lien heard the *black box*.   20

The friend turned the box on and Wu Lien heard sound coming from it. He knew what it was but he had never listened to one before. The box spoke music and news and the two men sat and listened to it most afternoons.

Wu Lien learned many things from this box but the most   25
important thing he learned was that there was war in other parts of the world. Others were suffering and fighting besides his country. Wu Lien decided that he must have a box of his own.

'Can you buy a box for me and I will hide it in my room?'   30
he asked his friend.

'It is dangerous, for you know you are not allowed to have

any of these boxes, but we are friends and I will try,' said the enemy scholar.

A few weeks later there was a knock on Wu Lien's door. He opened it and his enemy friend thrust* a parcel into
5 his hands. Wu Lien paid him a great deal of money for the box, then he set it to work and he listened to it every day and hid it under his bed at night.

One afternoon his cousin came with more information on Ling Tan and the village. Now this cousin was an unhappy
10 man for he did not want to tell Wu Lien anything about the village but his wife had started informing and she forced him to continue. Something else forced him to continue being an informer on his own people. Opium!

This cousin of Wu Lien's wife had grown to despise life
15 and took comfort in smoking opium. He told no one of this habit and the villagers thought his thin frame was from lack of food. He would take the money Wu Lien paid him and buy his peace in opium, telling his wife that Wu Lien was holding the money for them.

20 On this particular afternoon he was desperate for money to feed his habit. He surprised Wu Lien by arriving at the door of his rooms and thus the cousin saw the *black box* that told news.

'Don't ever tell anyone I have this box, cousin,' cried
25 Wu Lien.

'I won't,' the cousin said. Just then there was a knock on the door and Wu Lien was called to the lower part of the house.

'I will return in a few minutes,' he said and left his cousin
30 with the *black box*.

This cousin saw the answer to his problems in this box. He undid the wires, hid the box in his sack of vegetables, and left Wu Lien's rooms.

When he returned home he told his wife of his good for-
35 tune, lying and saying that Wu Lien gave him the box in

*thrust*, to push with force.

80

payment for his services as an informant. She was very happy and they planned to make money.

'But it is my box and I will listen and make people pay me for the world news, and, I will smoke a little opium, wife,' said the cousin with new-found confidence. She agreed,   *5* for what harm does a little smoke on occasion do to a man? They would make so much money from the box that a bit for opium would not be missed.

## News

Their business began with hope of riches. But a man does not smoke just a little opium on occasion, he must smoke it   *10* all the time. The routine began. The cousin would listen to the box, then sell the information to his countrymen who were eager for news. He would whisper it in their ears, take their money and go directly to the nearest opium house. His habit grew and grew and though he destroyed himself,   *15* he gave his people something that money could not buy. Hope.

The box told of a war in the whole world. In Ling Tan's house it was Lao Er who heard the news first and he ran all the way home from the city to tell his family.   *20*

'Our trouble is but part of a greater trouble and we are not suffering alone!' He cried as he spoke. They were tears of hope and inspiration. Soon the news spread through the whole village.

The news for the people was *resist*. There were others in   *25* the world suffering the same and worse than they and the box told all people who believed in a peaceful world, resist the enemy.

The village people heard the names of Germany and Italy and Canada and France. The world was now divided into   *30* friends and enemies depending on which side you and your people stood. It was somehow easier to eat their own miserable food when they knew there were others in the world who had no better. Best of all, they knew they were not alone and that many other nations hated the East Ocean devils just as they did.

Ling Tan listened to Lao Er's every word. 'So are there other devils besides the East Ocean ones?' he asked his son.

5     'Yes, and they do the same to those people and those people resist, father, as we do,' said Lao Er, excitedly.

'I wish I could know those people, they must be the ones on the other side of my land. The ones I was going to charge a rent for using the other end of my land,' he said, smiling.

10   'I won't charge them now, for they are the same as we are. No, they can use the other side of my land.' And he laughed for the first time in many months. The rest of the family laughed with him, remembering the old joke of better times.

He remembered that Jade had once told him that there

15   was only one moon and one sun for all. He had not believed her then, but now he did. 'If all of us who want peace in the world could unite, it would be a wonderful life,' he thought.

For the first time in his life Ling Tan had a feeling of the rest of the world. All this he learned from the news from

20   that little black box. 'There is hope for the world,' he thought happily. 'Hope is all we have.'

# 14
## Ling Tan and Wu Lien

Meanwhile the whole village wondered where Ling Tan's cousin was and why he did not come home. His wife came to Ling Tan and wept, begging him to find her man.

Ling Tan spoke to his family about this problem and it was decided that Lao Er would go to the city to see Wu Lien, for surely he would know where the cousin was.

One day in the ninth month of that year Lao Er went to Wu Lien's house, presenting himself as his brother-in-law. The soldiers took him to Wu Lien's rooms at the top of the grand staircase.

When Lao Er saw the fat, rich Wu Lien he was angry but he greeted him for fear of the enemy in the hall. 'Hello, brother-in-law, how are you? You certainly look fine,' he said coldly.

By now, Wu Lien was used to the anger of his people so he ignored the coldness. 'Yes, I am well. What can I do for you?' he asked.

Lao Er told him how the old cousin had disappeared and what a burden his wife was and asked him if anything could be done.

Wu Lien smiled, and in a small whisper he told Lao Er the whole truth of how the third cousin and his wife had been "his ears" in the village and how one day the cousin had come in and seen the foreign *black box* and had stolen it.

'He is in the city now,' said Wu Lien and he told Lao Er where the cousin was and what he was doing.

'I thought you were against us,' said Lao Er.

'I am against no one, least of all my wife's family,' he said. 'I told no one the news of the village but only hid it in my mind for myself.'

Lao Er was greatly relieved when he left Wu Lien. He

returned to the village and told the family his news and how their own cousin was an informer. Ling Tan had never liked that woman and now he hated her. The following day he and Lao Er went to the city to see this cousin for themselves.

### Their cousin

5   They found the tea-house and went inside. Ling Tan was shocked to see bold young women waiting on the tables but he kept quiet and waited for what Wu Lien had said would happen.

There before their eyes, at the appointed hour, a thin,
10  yellow man in a torn, purple robe came out from the back room of the tea-house.

'It is him. Our cousin,' whispered Lao Er.

'I see,' said Ling Tan, sadly.

The crowd came in from the street when they saw the
15  cousin come from the back room.

Their cousin's eyes were of another world as he began to speak in a quiet voice. 'You who hear me, the flying ships

84

have reached the capital. Oh, what sad news for us today.'
He rolled his eyes and said, 'I have the most evil news to tell
today. There is to be a puppet ruler* set up in this very city
who will rule for the enemy but in the name of our own
people, and we are to obey him and to pretend to do what
his choices are for us. Who is he? He is the "Three Drops of
Water King".'

At this news a great murmur* arose from the crowd.
The old cousin nodded and said, 'A very great evil, and tomorrow at this same hour I shall have more to tell you.'

The people who had listened to the cousin came forward
and gave him some coins. He bowed his head and returned
to the back room to ease the pain of life with his opium.

Ling Tan and Lao Er went out from the tea-house and
went home. Ling Tan thought of what his cousin had said;
how in this city there was to be set up a puppet, a man well
known among their own people. His anger rose at that weak
and handsome man who had betrayed his nation. 'Was it
betrayal or has he a trick in his mind?' thought Ling Tan.

The next morning when his cousin's wife came to Ling
Tan, he kept his face stern and told her a lie.

'Woman, what you feared is true. Your man is dead and
there is no body for you to bury. Ask me no more for I
will never tell you,' he said. He felt better knowing his cousin
would indeed be dead soon, and by telling the woman this
he would spare his cousin her wrath* in his last hours.

Lao Er told Jade everything and she was very grave when
she heard of this puppet ruler.

'We will have to wait and see what he does,' said Lao
Er.

'Yes, and we will continue to resist!' cried Jade.

*puppet ruler, someone who seems to rule by himself but is ordered to do things
by someone else. *murmur, a low continous sound of voices when words are not
clear. *wrath, anger.

## *15*
## *Lao San*

The hill men and the young and the old everywhere waged their secret war against the enemy.

Again, when the harvest came that year, Ling Tan had to sell his rice at the enemy's fixed prices. Again he ate his meat secretly. The taxes were great but the farmers still hid a great    5
deal of the grain from the enemy.

In the midst of all this Jade and Lao Er expected their second child and Lao Er went on with his work between the city and the country.

What Lao Er did was to come and go between the guerillas*    10
living in or near the city, who were farmers by day, and those men in the hills, so that they could meet together to plan their strikes against the enemy.

He was clever at passing by the enemy in the many disguises which Jade created for him.    15

### *Lao San*

The youngest of Ling Tan's sons, Lao San, now wore a uniform such as soldiers wear and his mind was always on war and death. He still could not read a word, and for him books were evil and learning was evil. All was evil except the simple force in his right arm when it lifted a sword or shot    20
a gun. These days he lived in a temple in the hills which he made into a fortress, and with two hundred and fifty young men under him, he went out from there to strike and strike again.

Every look of the slender boy, whom once the enemy had    25
used, had now gone from him. He had grown taller and his eyes were like a tiger's. No woman alive could pass by him

---

*guerrillas, small groups of fighting men, not belonging to the official army.

without wanting him in some way and this he knew but he did not care.

He was nineteen now. His desires grew in him and even the men in his band knew that Lao San needed a woman. But he
5  found none who interested him for he needed more than a body, he needed a woman with a spirit to match his own. Sometimes when his desire grew great, his temper would erupt* and his men suffered until he could attack the enemy to rid his body of this energy.

10  One day when Lao Er came up to the hills to see Lao San, one of Lao San's men drew him aside. 'Please, Lao Er,' said the warrior, 'your brother needs a woman. A wife.'

'I know, but who in these times? The women are hidden or have been used!' answered Lao Er.

15  But the young man had put the thought in his mind and he thought of it as he travelled home to the village. 'Who could marry him? She would have to be so beautiful, but with spirit and life in her.'

When he arrived home he mentioned this to his father.

20  'But who can we find for that man?' asked Ling Tan.

'I don't know,' said Lao Er. 'But he needs a woman.'

Ling Sao had been listening and now she dared to speak of an idea she had had in her mind for many months. 'Let us go and ask the white woman if we can write to our daughter,
25  Pansiao, and ask her to find a virgin for Lao San from her school.' The men turned and stared at Ling Sao for the idea was a good one.

'A fine idea,' said Ling Tan. 'I will go and see the white woman tomorrow.'

### A letter to Pansiao

30  The following day Ling Tan went to the city and found his way to the white woman's house. He knocked on the gate and asked the gateman if he could speak to the white woman.

*erupt*, break through.

'You have not heard, then?' asked the gateman.

'Heard what?' said Ling Tan.

'She is dead. The white woman is dead. She took her own life and left a letter saying she was sorry she had failed her mission,' the gateman said sadly.

Ling Tan was sad to hear of this for he knew this white woman was a good woman. 'But how can I write to my daughter?' he asked.

'Go and write the letter and I will see that it is taken by someone to her school,' said the gateman.

Ling Tan returned home and told his family what had happened to the white woman. They were all sad and they agreed that she was a good and kind soul.

'Now Jade must write the letter to Pansiao and tell her to find Lao San a beautiful, virgin wife with a strong spirit and a kind nature,' said Ling Sao.

They all laughed and Ling Tan said, 'Woman, you ask for a goddess!'

'Yes, he needs a goddess,' said Ling Sao. 'Jade, tell Pansiao to find her brother a goddess for none other could hold him and tame his spirit.'

Jade wrote the letter and when she had finished she read it out to the family and they all marvelled at her beautiful words.

'But where on earth will Pansiao find her brother a living goddess?' she thought as she gave the letter to Ling Tan.

# *16*
## *The Goddess*

In her own small part of the cave Pansiao sat with her back
to the others and read the letter which Jade had written. Two
thousand miles away Jade had written the letter and by the
time it reached Pansiao it was winter again.

5       She folded the letter slowly when she had read it and put
each fold in its place. 'How can I find a wife for my brother?
Particularly *this* brother!' she thought.

For Pansiao knew her family very well. All through those
years when she sat at the loom and moved about the house
10    quietly, she had learned a skill; the skill of watching. She
had watched them all and so she knew them under their skin
for they had not noticed her watching them and so they had
been themselves in front of her. Now she thought of Lao San
and she could imagine the great and strong leader he had
15    become. They had been closest in age and she knew him
so very well.

She put the letter away and looked around her. There were
twelve girls in the school in the cave. Some were pretty, to be
sure and some were bright in their schoolwork. But she could
20    send none of these home for Lao San, though she knew they
would all willingly have become his wife. But they were not
for him and Pansiao knew this in her heart. As she looked
around for a goddess, she saw none.

For days she thought of nothing else but finding the
25    goddess for Lao San. She always came back to the same
thought. What girl do I know who is strong enough to hold
my brother? And the answer was always the same. None.


*Mayli*
But at this very moment there was a woman coming near
to Pansiao's mountain-school. This woman had come many

thousands of miles from a foreign country to this country of her own which she did not remember. Her father had taken her away years ago and in this foreign country she had grown into womanhood. She was not yet nineteen and her mother was dead. 5

Her father had not wanted her to return to their country. He had been angry when she had told him of her plans. But he knew she was a strong girl and had grown up in a free country and she would go if she wanted. The girl's name was Mayli and she was beautiful. She had a strain* of Arab 10 blood in her Chinese veins and this darkness made her more beautiful.

'But father, I cannot stay here in safety and be happy when the East Ocean people are taking our country,' she had told her father. 15

'But what will you do in a war?' he had asked.

'I will teach,' she announced and she made her plans to go back to the country of her birth, where her mother had died giving her life.

She had agreed to her father's request that she should 20 teach in a mission school. The Chinese Embassy had been only too happy to see a former native returning home and they gave her a visa.

Thus the beautiful and wilful Mayli came to Pansiao's school one cold, clear morning two months after her decision 25 to help her home country in war-time.

Mayli entered the school grounds and a servant led her to the headmistress' office.

When the door was opened Mayli saw a stern, plain, white woman sitting behind the desk. 30

'Are you Miss Freem?' asked Mayli.

'Yes, welcome,' she said.

Mayli thought immediately, 'I won't like this woman.'

And Miss Freem immediately thought, 'I shall have trouble with this bold-looking girl.' 35

*strain (of Arab blood), someone in her family's history was an Arab.

91

That was how their relationship began. Each woman was
cautious of the other before they had spoken more than ten
words to each other.

For two hours Miss Freem explained the school policy to
5 Mayli. Then she took her around to meet the students and
see the rest of the mission school.

When Mayli entered the classroom, a wave of excitement
rose in the girls. Pansiao was overcome with Mayli's beauty.

'This is our new teacher?' she said to the girl sitting next to her. 'She is one of us,' she thought. Then, she heard Mayli speak English to Miss Freem and she was truly shocked that a Chinese girl could speak it as though it were her own language.

Suddenly Mayli spoke to the class in Chinese and the girls were shocked again.

Pansiao wanted to shout out, 'The Goddess. This is my

5

goddess for Lao San.' But she would never do anything of the sort and it was a silly thought, she knew. The thought would not leave her mind as she watched the beautiful, new teacher leave the classroom. And she thought of nothing else
5 for the rest of that day.

The next day Mayli taught her first class and Pansiao could not stop staring at her beauty. And now she knew her strength, for Mayli spoke in a strong, confident voice.

It was time for reading and Pansiao took out the reading
10 book that Miss Freem had assigned the girls.

Mayli walked by Pansiao's desk and looking down she exclaimed, ' "Paul Revere's Ride!". '

Pansiao had not understood what the goddess said for she spoke in English but she did understand the look of dis-
15 approval on her face. Pansiao took this disapproval personally.

Mayli asked Pansiao a few questions and Pansiao told her that she and the other girls had to memorize the text. Mayli was disgusted with this form of learning.

'Why aren't they reading of their own culture?' she
20 thought. And then she went directly to Miss Freem's office.

She burst into the office saying, 'I don't understand, Miss Freem. Memorizing "Paul Revere's Ride", serves these girls no purpose. It must stop.'

Miss Freem was shocked. This new teacher of less than
25 nineteen was telling her how to run her school. 'God, deliver me from this girl,' thought the angry headmistress. 'We will discuss this later, Mayli,' said Miss Freem in an icy voice.

Mayli knew the conversation was over and she returned to her class, boiling with anger.

30 Mayli noticed Pansiao waiting for her at the end of class. 'What is it child, what can I do for you?' she asked.

'I'm sorry if my work displeased you,' said the timid* Pansiao.

'Oh, no, your work didn't displease me. It was something
35 else,' answered Mayli. She looked at Pansiao's eager face and

---

*timid*, easily frightened.

94

sensed she wanted to say something more. 'What is it?' she said, softly.

In her simple way she told Mayli the story of her home and she even told her of her sister's husband, Wu Lien. And she told her about her brothers and then she finally said, 'Will you marry my brother?' 5

Mayli wanted to laugh but she didn't want to hurt Pansiao's feelings. 'Thank you for the offer but I don't wish to marry, now.' She saw the girl's face fall in dismay so to humour* her she asked her about her brother. 10

'He is beautiful and strong and he fights the enemy from the East Ocean. And no woman can hold him although they all want him.' She talked on and on of Lao San.

And Mayli, who had asked about him to merely humour the girl, was fascinated with what she said. 'If one half she 15 says is true, I would like to meet this Lao San,' she thought, smiling.

That evening Mayli could not clear her mind of the things Pansiao said. Pansiao's city was the city of Mayli's mother. She tossed and turned in her bed as visions of Lao San went 20 through her mind.

'I must not be romantic,' she thought. 'I can tell I'm not happy in this school, already, but I must stop thinking of this man I've never even met. I must not be a fool,' she said to herself and she went to sleep. 25

*to humour, to satisfy a person's needs.

# 17
# The Journey

Mayli avoided Pansiao for days and when by chance she saw her, she smiled quickly and looked away.

She was also troubled by other feelings. 'I was never meant to be a school teacher,' she thought passionately. 'I can't
5    even sing hymns!'

Yet what was she meant to be? She now asked herself that constantly. What could a woman do alone? What if she sent for the pilot who had brought her here and told him to take her — anywhere? But where would she go?

10    Meanwhile, Miss Freem thought, 'I shall have to do something about that girl. She is like a tiger. Oh, God, please let me find a way to get rid of her!'

And it was Mayli who thought, 'I must get out of here.'

And Miss Freem set her free.

15    'God gave me the strength,' she said to the other teachers when the deed was done. 'I called her to my office and said, "Miss Wei, I consider that your contract at this school is broken!"'

Mayli was thrilled with Miss Freem's decision. She de-
20    manded her full salary and she sent a telegram to the nearest city. In a few days the pilot arrived and Mayli left the mission school without even a farewell to Pansiao.

When Pansiao found that her goddess had gone she wept and wept for days.

25    Mayli felt free and she had money in her pocket and a wild plan in her heart. She would go and see for herself if that brother were as handsome as Pansiao claimed he was. And she would visit the city and find her mother's grave.

Now Mayli was one of those women who had never seen
30    a man she thought was her equal. She was scornful of men yet she was a passionate woman and Pansiao's brother sounded wild and untamed. She imagined him as her dragon,

96

stronger than she was and yet dependent on her for learning. She wanted him untamed, and yet she wanted to shape him.

So, she plotted and planned how to get close enough to this man to see him and know whether or not she wanted him.                                                                     5

The plan was not too hard. She saw a very clear way if she chose to take it. Pansiao had given her enough information to help her along the way. She knew of Wu Lien, the brother-in-law who worked for the new government of the puppet. The 10 puppet had once been her father's friend, and she had known him in the days when the country was free. He had always been a rebel and had spent many years abroad in exile and that was how Mayli's father knew him. She would write to the puppet and then go to visit him and find this Wu Lien 15 who would surely lead her to Lao San.

## Mayli and the puppet

Mayli did as she planned and sent a telegram to the puppet. Within a few hours there was his message, begging her to come and visit him. He would provide protection for her on her journey and she would stay in his fine house.                            20

Secretly, she hated this puppet but she would use him. The thought of him living in a fine house when his countrymen were starving made her ill.

Two days later she arrived in the city and the puppet, himself, greeted her.                                                                                      25

'I am lonely,' he told her, and she knew he wanted her. But she had no intention* of giving herself to him.

'Ah, Mayli, you understand me. I am not a traitor. I am a realist. If you recognize the truth, that these East Ocean people have conquered all our country, the only hope for our 30 future is to work with them. Besides, what I'm doing is very Chinese. Our history tells us that we have always seemed to

---

*intention, the plan in a person's mind to do something.

yield to our conquerors, but actually we have ruled and they have died.'

She listened and held her tongue for once. She wanted to scream, 'Weakling!' at him but she dared not. There was a
5 knock on the door and a fat man in a fine silk robe entered.

'Mayli, this is Wu Lien. He is my secretary and very faithful to me.'

So that brother-in-law had risen as high as this among the enemy, and this made it all the easier for her to fulfill her
10 plan.

Wu Lien carried some news for the puppet and the two men spoke in low voices in front of Mayli.

When they finished speaking Mayli asked a question. 'I wonder, sir, if someone that you trust would take me out
15 into the countryside to visit my mother's grave?' she said, smiling at the puppet and Wu Lien.

'Allow me,' cried Wu Lien attempting to please the puppet.

'Oh, sir, that would be wonderful,' said Mayli, before the puppet had even a chance to think about the offer.
20 'Tomorrow?' asked Mayli in her sweetest voice.

And the two men who had long since seen a beautiful woman, and especially one as beautiful as Mayli, melted under her gaze.

'Tomorrow is fine,' said the puppet, weakly.
25 Mayli smiled at them both.

## 18
## The Match

Now on that day Ling Tan sat on a bench and mended the yoke* for his buffalo. He was weary because he had been sleepless most of the night. There had been two days and nights of danger. His eldest son had come to warn him that the men of the hills were planning to attack and wipe out an  5 entire garrison* of the enemy. And so they did and Ling Tan knew his youngest son had led the attack.

They had won and at this very moment Ling Tan's two sons lay sleeping in his house, weary with what they had been through. The third son had a small wound in his arm.  10

So, although on this morning Ling Tan looked like a peaceful old farmer, he was very uneasy and he watched all who came and went near him.

As he lifted his eyes to search the road he saw Wu Lien and his daughter coming towards him with their children. When  15 they came near enough to him he saw that they had a stranger with them; a woman young and tall and more foreign in her looks than any woman he had ever seen that he took her to be one of the enemy women.

He did not rise when they came near but he greeted them  20 pleasantly.

'Here we are, my father. Here are the children,' said his daughter. 'And this is a friend who visits those above us. She has come to look for her mother's grave in the Mohammedan burial-ground.'  25

Ling Tan then knew that this was no enemy woman. He rose and said to Mayli, 'I thought you were an enemy, because you look so foreign, but if you are a Mohammedan that is why you look the way you do.'

---

*yoke, a piece of wood fastened over the neck of buffalo attached to something which is to be pulled. *garrison, group of soldiers living in a town to defend it.

She smiled at the old farmer.

Suddenly, Ling Tan's third son came through the gate to relieve himself of water. He did not see the visitors.

'Stop it. There is a stranger here,' cried Ling Tan.

5 Lao San turned and was so ashamed that he ran into the house. He stopped to catch his breath but it was not the running that had taken it away. The moment Lao San put his eyes on Mayli he saw her black shining hair and her red cheeks and her full lips and her white teeth, and his heart
10 almost stopped for he had never seen a woman so beautiful. But he was ashamed of what he had done and so he hid in the house.

'Was that not my third brother?' cried Ling Tan's daughter.

15 Then Ling Tan did what he would never have dreamed he could. He fell on his knees before Wu Lien because he knew their lives were in his hands.

Wu Lien turned to his wife and said, 'I did not see anyone.' He pulled Ling Tan to his feet and repeated, 'I did not see
20 anyone!'

Ling Tan said, 'Thank you.' Then he asked them to come into his house.

Mayli saw this family gathering before her eyes, and they were all as Pansiao had told her. She listened to them and
25 looked at them, smiling and silent. She saw Jade come out, heavy with child, and Mayli liked her because Jade was not shy.

'Tell your sons to come out, Ling Sao,' said Ling Tan.

At this the eldest son came, shy and quiet but that third
30 son would not come out. He sat inside his room and he cursed himself for what he had done in front of this woman.

Ling Sao went to his room and grabbed him by the ear and said, 'Your father says you must come out and I don't care if you are a great fighter, you are still his son and you will do as
35 he says!'

Lao San entered the courtyard with his eyes to the ground. But they would not stay there for he had to look up at the woman before him. He thought, 'I never dreamed to see a woman like this.'

Their eyes met and then Mayli quickly turned to Wu Lien and said, 'I want to go to the grave now.'

Mayli rose and thanked Ling Tan and waited outside the 5 gate for Wu Lien. He joined her and off they went in the direction of the burial-ground.

Now when Ling Tan came back to his seat, he saw that his third son wanted to speak to him.

'What is it, Lao San?' he asked. 10

'That woman,' he said, quietly.

'What woman? The foreigner?'

'Yes,' he said. 'Get her for my wife.'

When Ling Tan heard this he went red with anger. 'Ling Sao,' he yelled. 'Come here.' 15

Ling Sao knew her man and she knew the tone of anger in his voice. 'Yes, husband, what is it?'

'It's this son of yours! He thinks he made heaven and earth,' yelled Ling Tan.

Ling Sao did not understand the trouble, and she repeated, 20 'What is it. What is wrong?'

'This third son of yours, the one who said he wouldn't marry any woman. Now he wants the foreign woman and he wants me to get her for him,' screamed Ling Tan.

Suddenly, Lao San could bear this no longer. 'I am not a 25 child, father. I am a man. I must go away from this house!' He said, losing his temper.

Ling Tan let him go and Ling Sao fretted after him but he went anyway. And everyone in the family knew he would return when his temper had cooled. 30

'Oh, wife, if I could get that woman for him, I would. But she is a rich foreigner and what can I offer her but the boy, himself. This is why I am so angry for he asks me to do the impossible for him!'

'Maybe it is not so impossible,' said Ling Sao and she ran 35 to the gate and called to her daughter, Wu Lien's wife, who had not wanted to go to a burial-ground and so she had stayed in the back room with the others.

Ling Sao told her what Lao San wanted.

'I will do what I can, mother, but I doubt that the foreign woman would want him,' she said.

## Love

5 Now Lao San went straight to the burial-ground and crept in the grass so none would see him. From where he lay he could see her in all her glory and he loved her more. Then he stood to watch her for he wanted her to see him there, but she would not look up and he liked this, too.

10 Jade had gone to tell Lao Er all the news of Lao San and the woman. 'It's the goddess,' she cried. 'She is the goddess for Lao San.'

'But they are so different,' said Lao Er.

Jade smiled and said, 'Are they?'. She had watched the
15 foreign woman and she saw the spirit in her heart. 'But how to get the two together?' she wondered.

## Together

Mayli went straight to her room in the puppet's house and threw off her cloak. The morning had made her heart soft. His face was imprinted in her mind and heart. Whoever he
20 was, he was brave and very beautiful and there was power in him. Yet she knew she could never live in Ling Tan's house. 'We will go away together to another place, and forsake* all others but ourselves,' she thought. 'We could go to the free land and join our power together and we can visit the
25 family once in a while but we won't live there — ever.'

Everyone in Ling Tan's house tried to think of ways to bring Lao San and this goddess together. But it was Mayli herself who did it all.

She waited for two days then she returned, alone, to Ling

*forsake*, give up something; take away help or friendship from someone.

102

Tan's house. And she asked for Jade.

Jade let her in the gate and Mayli sat down.

'I have come back to tell you that I know Pansiao. I was her teacher in the mountains,' said Mayli. She told Jade the whole story and that she had read the letter. 5

'I knew it,' cried Jade. 'I knew you were our goddess.'

Mayli smiled and said, 'Here, I want you to give this to Lao San.' She handed Jade the forbidden silk flag of the free people; blue and red with the sun upon it. 'Tell him I am going to the free lands. I will wait for him there.' She held 10 Jade's hand and said, 'I go to Kunming and he will come.'

Of this, Jade had no doubt.

## 19
## A Little Happiness

When Mayli left Ling Tan's home, Jade went and told the others her news. Ling Tan and Ling Sao were happy that their son would be with the woman he loved.

It was all new to Ling Tan. 'My son will go after a woman?
5 The woman always comes to the man,' he said out loud. But so many things had changed since the enemy had come, and this was just one more change in his life.

The family waited for the birth of Lao Er's child and it would be a large child for Jade was carrying a heavy load.

10 In all the excitement over the woman and the third son, everyone forgot the loneliness of Lao Ta, the eldest. He had never found another woman after Orchid and everyone could see it in the sadness of his face.

There were so few women about that were available to
15 marry and Lao Ta knew this and it depressed him. He threw himself into his work, both on the farm and in the hills. He was an expert at trapping* the enemy and he knew how to build the very best of traps. One day when he least expected it, he trapped himself a woman.

20 He had dug the trap in the road the night before and carefully laid grass and bamboo over the hole. When he returned the next morning he did not find an enemy in the hole. He found a crying woman.

'Help me!' she cried when she looked up and saw Lao Ta
25 standing above the hole.

He had pulled her up and felt her warmth. 'I am sorry. I was trying to catch the enemy, not you,' he said.

She told him her story of how the enemy had killed her husband and children and now she was looking for the village
30 of his people. Lao Ta's heart went out to her for he knew her

*trapping, making traps; using a trick to catch someone.

104

pain was his pain. His wife and children had also died.

'Come home to my parents' house for some food,' he said.

She followed him home and the two talked the whole way.

He took her through the gate to meet Ling Sao. But Ling Sao cried, 'I have no time to meet women, Jade is having trouble with the baby.'

The woman said, 'I have delivered many babies, let me help.'

Ling Sao led her to Jade's room and there the woman took command. 'I feel a boy's head,' said the woman and in a few minutes she pulled the boy from Jade.

Ling Sao cried, 'It's a son,' and took the child in her arms.

'Wait, for there is to be another,' said the woman as she wiped Jade's head with a cool cloth. And in another while, the second boy was born.

Ling Sao wept for joy and told all the news. Lao Er came and held Jade close to him to comfort her and share in the birth of their twin sons.

Soon all the village rejoiced in the births, for they had had too much sadness and pain and nothing is so wonderful as new life.

Ling Tan and Ling Sao thanked the woman. Lao Ta told them her story and they saw joy on his face.

Soon there was more happiness for in a week's time Lao Ta and the woman were married.

*Hope*

Lao San had gone with his Mayli but Ling Tan's house was full again and in this he was pleased.

The enemy still ruled and as far as he could see, it would go on. He bore* their cruel taxes and their unjust greed. He felt anger over the open sale of opium in the city and watched many fall victim to its evil.

Ling Tan watched the enemy take anything they wanted

*bore*, accepted without complaint.

and ship it back to that cursed country of theirs. 'The earth is one thing they cannot ship back,' he would think, and smile to himself.

But he was losing hope and that is the worst thing a man
5 can have happen to his spirit. For by now he had heard that none of the countries of the world had come forward to stand at their side or to give them aid. The countries sold their guns to the highest bidders and more often than not his country's bid was the lowest.

10 As Ling Tan's sixtieth birthday approached, Ling Sao worried about her husband and she begged her son to take him to a tea-house in the city, just to get away from the farm for an afternoon.

So Lao Er took Ling Tan to the tea-house and there was
15 their cousin, still alive but thinner and drowsier than ever.

The cousin came out to read his news and all went quiet in the tea-house. 'Friends, I tell you today of a meeting between the man from the country of Mei and the other from Ying. And today the one from Ying has spoken. He has
20 said that we must resist for we are united now and there will be more suffering but there is light now at the end of this tunnel.'

And the others in the tea-house told of what they had heard of this man and the meeting.

25 Ling Tan drank in every word and then he felt the tears come up into his eyes. All through the bitter years he had not wept. He had seen ruin in his home and in his village, and he had seen death everywhere, but he had not wept. This was the first good news that any one had given him in more than
30 four years and he wept.

'Let us go,' he said to his son.

So his son followed him and they went out from the city and Ling Tan said nothing.

Then Ling Tan stopped on the dark road and looked up at
35 the sky. He looked at the stars and lifted his hand to feel the wind. 'Is there not a promise of rain?' Ling Tan said.

'Only a promise,' answered Lao Er.

# Questions

## 1
## Ling Tan and his Family

A.  Describe Ling Tan's family and home.
B.  What kind of man is Ling Tan?
C.  Why is talking so important to Jade?

## 2
## A Journey to the City

A.  Why was Lao Er ashamed on the booksellers' street?
B.  Why was Wu Lien's shop attacked?
C.  If you were Lao Er and saw the state the shop was in, would you have gone inside to see your family? Explain your answer.

## 3
## The Land

A.  What was Ling Tan's attitude toward his land?
B.  What was Wu Lien trying to tell his wife and Ling Sao?
C.  How did Ling Sao feel when she left Wu Lien's house? Why?

## 4
## The Flying Ships

A.  Why didn't the farmers hide from the flying ships?
B.  Would you have hidden? Explain.
C.  Describe exactly what Ling Tan and his son found in the city.

## 5
## The Beginning

A. Where did the people of the city go?
B. If you were Ling Tan would you have stayed or left? Explain.

## 6
## Waiting for the Enemy

A. Describe Ling Tan's meeting with the enemy.
B. Contrast Ling Tan's feelings at the beginning and then the end of this chapter. Use examples in your description.

## 7
## The White Woman and her House

A. Who was the white woman and what was her profession?
B. Why did Ling Sao fear the white woman?

## 8
## The East Ocean Enemy

A. What does Wu Lien do with the enemy? Do you agree or disagree with his actions? Explain your answer.
B. What happens to change Lao San's life forever?

## 9
## Wu Lien and the Enemy

A. Wu Lien makes a choice in this chapter. Would you agree with his choice? Explain.
B. What happens to Orchid in this chapter?

## 10
## Letters

A. Historically, who are the East Ocean devils?
B. What happens to Lao Er and Jade in this chapter? Would you make the same choice as Lao Er?

# 11
## Resistance

A. How did Ling Tan and the other farmers quietly resist the enemy? Describe what they did?

B. Why didn't the enemy kill them for their actions?

# 12
## The Secret War

A. Describe the secret war in detail.

# 13
## The Whole World

A. What is the *black box* and how did the people learn about the world from it?

# 14
## Ling Tan and Wu Lien

A. What happened to Ling Tan's cousin?

B. Why did Ling Tan tell his cousin's wife he was dead?

C. Imagine you and your partner are Ling Tan and his cousin's wife. Act out the conversation they would have.

# 15
## Lao San

A. Why was Lao San so ill-tempered?

B. What did Jade write to Pansiao?

# 16
## The Goddess

A. Who was Mayli and where did she come from?

B. What did Pansiao tell Mayli?

# 17
## The Journey

A.  Who was the puppet?
B.  How did Mayli know him?

# 18
## The Match

A.  What happened when Mayli and Lao San met?
B.  Where did they go?

# 19
## A Little Happiness

A.  What happened to Lao Ta?
B.  What joy happened to Lao Er and Jade?
C.  Why did Ling Tan weep at the end of the story?

# Oxford Progressive English Readers

## Introductory Grade

Vocabulary restricted to 1400 headwords
Illustrated in full colour

| | |
|---|---|
| The Call of the Wild and Other Stories | Jack London |
| Emma | Jane Austen |
| Jungle Book Stories | Rudyard Kipling |
| Life Without Katy and Seven Other Stories | O. Henry |
| Little Women | Louisa M. Alcott |
| The Lost Umbrella of Kim Chu | Eleanor Estes |
| Stories from Vanity Fair | W.M. Thackeray |
| Tales from the Arabian Nights | Retold by Rosemary Border |
| Treasure Island | R.L. Stevenson |

## Grade 1

Vocabulary restricted to 2100 headwords
Illustrated in full colour

| | |
|---|---|
| The Adventures of Sherlock Holmes | Sir Arthur Conan Doyle |
| Alice's Adventures in Wonderland | Lewis Carroll |
| A Christmas Carol | Charles Dickens |
| Great Expectations | Charles Dickens |
| Gulliver's Travels | Jonathan Swift |
| Hijacked! | J.M. Marks |
| Jane Eyre | Charlotte Brontë |
| Lord Jim | Joseph Conrad |
| Oliver Twist | Charles Dickens |
| The Stone Junk | Retold by D.H. Howe |
| Stories of Shakespeare's Plays 1 | Retold by N. Kates |
| Tales from Tolstoy | Retold by R.D. Binfield |
| The Talking Tree and Other Stories | David McRobbie |

## Grade 2

Vocabulary restricted to 3100 headwords
Illustrated in colour

| | |
|---|---|
| The Adventures of Tom Sawyer | Mark Twain |
| Alice's Adventures Through the Looking Glass | Lewis Carroll |
| Around the World in Eighty Days | Jules Verne |
| Border Kidnap | J.M. Marks |
| David Copperfield | Charles Dickens |
| Five Tales | Oscar Wilde |
| Fog and Other Stories | Bill Lowe |
| Further Adventures of Sherlock Holmes | Sir Arthur Conan Doyle |
| The Hound of the Baskervilles | Sir Arthur Conan Doyle |
| The Missing Scientist | S.F. Stevens |

## Grade 2 (cont.)

| | |
|---|---|
| The Red Badge of Courage | Stephen Crane |
| Robinson Crusoe | Daniel Defoe |
| Seven Chinese Stories | T.J. Sheridan |
| Stories of Shakespeare's Plays 2 | Retold by Wyatt & Fullerton |
| A Tale of Two Cities | Charles Dickens |
| Tales of Crime and Detection | Retold by G.F. Wear |
| Two Boxes of Gold and Other Stories | Charles Dickens |

## Grade 3

Vocabulary restricted to 3700 headwords
Illustrated in colour

| | |
|---|---|
| Battle of Wits at Crimson Cliff | Retold by Benjamin Chia |
| Dr Jekyll and Mr Hyde and Other Stories | R.L. Stevenson |
| From Russia, with Love | Ian Fleming |
| The Gifts and Other Stories | O. Henry & Others |
| The Good Earth | Pearl S. Buck |
| Journey to the Centre of the Earth | Jules Verne |
| Kidnapped | R.L. Stevenson |
| King Solomon's Mines | H. Rider Haggard |
| Lady Precious Stream | S.I. Hsiung |
| The Light of Day | Eric Ambler |
| Moonraker | Ian Fleming |
| The Moonstone | Wilkie Collins |
| A Night of Terror and Other Strange Tales | Guy De Maupassant |
| Seven Stories | H.G. Wells |
| Stories of Shakespeare's Plays 3 | Retold by H.G. Wyatt |
| Tales of Mystery and Imagination | Edgar Allan Poe |
| The War of the Worlds | H.G. Wells |
| 20,000 Leagues Under the Sea | Jules Verne |
| The Woman in White | Wilkie Collins |
| Wuthering Heights | Emily Brontë |
| You Only Live Twice | Ian Fleming |

## Grade 4

Vocabulary within a 5000 headwords range
Illustrated in black and white

| | |
|---|---|
| The Diamond as Big as the Ritz and Other Stories | F. Scott Fitzgerald |
| Dragon Seed | Pearl S. Buck |
| Frankenstein | Mary Shelley |
| The Mayor of Casterbridge | Thomas Hardy |
| Prelude and Other Stories | D.H. Lawrence |
| Pride and Prejudice | Jane Austen |
| The Stalled Ox and Other Stories | Saki |

This I